BROADSIDES
OF THE
INDUSTRIAL NORTH

by

MARTHA VICINUS
VICTORIAN STUDIES
INDIANA UNIVERSITY
BALLANTINE HALL 338
BLOOMINGTON, INDIANA 47401

Published by FRANK GRAHAM
6 Queen's Terrace, Newcastle upon Tyne, NE2 2PL

Printed by Howe Brothers (Gateshead) Ltd.

1975

I.S.B.N. 0 85983 063 2

ACKNOWLEDGEMENTS

I would like to thank the following libraries for permission to reproduce broadsides in their collections: The Sheffield City Libraries for 1, 3, 4, 10, 19 and 20; the British Library for 2, 41 and 44; the District Central Library (Preston) for 5, 6, 7, 11, 13, 36, 40, 45, 49, 51, 52 and 53; the Manchester Public Libraries for 8, 12 and 15; Chetham's Library, Manchester, for 9 and 46; Harvard College Library for 14; the Bradford City Central Library for 16, 17, 18, 37, 42 and 47; the University of Newcastle upon Tyne Library for 21, 22, 25, 32, 33, 38, 48 and 50; the Newcastle upon Tyne City Libraries for 23, 34 and 35; the Wigan City Library for 24; the Barnsley Libraries for 26, 27, 28 and 54; the South Shields Library for 29 and 31; the Liverpool City Libraries for 30; and the John Johnson Collection, Bodleian Library, Oxford University, for 39 and 43. I am grateful for their kindness in giving me permission. Portions of the introduction have appeared in *The Industrial Muse: A Study of Nineteenth Century British Working-Class Literature* (London: Croom Helm, 1974). I am grateful for permission from Croom Helm, Ltd., to reprint this material.

TABLE OF CONTENTS

26. "South Yorkshire Lock-Out. Barnsley Collieries" (no place, no publisher) [Barnsley] [7¼" x 4¾"]

27. "The Great Lock-out of Miners at Barnsley: New Song" (no place [Barnsley]: Witham's) [7½" x 5"]

28. "A Miners' Hymn" (Barnsley: J. Elliott) [8" x 5¼"]

29. "To the Public" (South Shields: R. M. Kelly, n.d. [1842]) [12¾" x 8"]

30. "A New Song on the Turn-out" (Liverpool: McCall) [9¾" x 7¾"]

31. "Sold Here, Corvan's Popular Songs" (Newcastle: W. Stewart) [11" x 4"]

32. "The Toon Improvement Bill; or Nee Pleyce Noo to Play" (Newcastle: W. Stewart) [by Ned Corvan] [11⅛" x 4½"]

33. "The Factory Lass, or Pally Jones" (Newcastle: W. Stewart) [by Ned Corvan] [11⅛" x 4½"]

34. "The Greet Strike, or The Nine Oors Movement" (Newcastle: T. Allan) [by Joe Wilson] [9⅝" x 7½"]

35. "We'll Seun Heh Wark Te De! or The Strike o' '71" (Newcastle: Thos. Allen) [by Joe Wilson] [8½" x 5⅜"]

36. "The Girls of Lancashire," "With My Jug in One Hand" and "And Home I Came Merrily at Last" (Preston: Harkness) [10" x 7⅜"]

37. "Steam Boots" and "Banks of Inverary" (Bradford: Spencer) [10⅜" x 7¾"]

38. "The Collier Swell" and "Annie Laurie" (Durham: Walker) [8⅞" x 6¾"]

39. "We'll Ride the Waves Triumphant" and "Slap-up Lodgings" (Manchester: Bebbington; Leeds: J. Beaumont) [9½" x 6½"]

40. "The Devil's in the Girl" (no place, no publisher) [9¾" x 4⅛"]

41. "Come Mary Link thi Arm i' Mine" (London: H. P. Such) [10" x 7⅜"]

42. "You Don't Know What You Can Do Till You Try" (Birmingham: T. King) [10" x 7½"]

43. "My Wife's First Baby" (no place, no publisher) [10½" x 7½"]

44. "Fifteen Shillings a Week" and "Mary Machree" (no place, no publisher) [10" x 7"]

45. "The Pawnbroker's Shop" (Preston: John Harkness) [9½" x 7"]

46. "Esmeralda" and "Do Everyone As You Can!" (Manchester: T. Pearson) [9¾" x 7¼"]

47. "Father, Dear Father," "Reply of the Father," "No Home Like the Drunkards," "The Bradford Chimney Disaster" (Heckmondwike: Joseph Ellis) [9¾" x 7¾"]

48. "Newcastle Town Moor Amusements at Whitsuntide" (Newcastle: Marshall) [13" x 5¼"]

49. "Never Maids Wed An Old Man" and "The Guild" (no place, no publisher) [10" x 6⅞"]

50. "Newcastle and London Boat Match for £100 A Side" (Newcastle: T. Dodds) [9¾" x 6⅝"]

51. "The Indian Maid," "Steer My Bark" and "He's Got No Courage in Him" (no place, no publisher) [9⅝" x 6⅝"]

52. "A Copy of Verses on the Sorrowful Lamentation of Thomas Stew" (Preston: Harkness) [9⅝" x 7"]

53. "The Cruel Sea Captain and Nancy of Yarmouth" and "Farwell to Your Judges and Juries" (Preston: John Harkness) [9⅝" x 6⅝"]

54. "The Pit Boy" (no place, no publisher [Barnsley]) [8" x 5¼"]

BROADSIDES OF THE INDUSTRIAL NORTH

In the 1890's a Manchester business man, Fred Leary, began a commonplace book in which he wrote his impressions of Manchester's popular culture—the songs of the music halls and taverns, the ballads offered by street 'chaunters' and the penny dreadfuls sold in shops and news stands. He purchased or copied out the songs he heard, with a description of the singer, and attempted to identify the age of the song. Leary justified his research as essential for understanding the culture and leisure pursuits of the working people of an industrial city:

> It must be of much importance to know of the character of that class of ballads which were manufactured for the working class—if those songs which in order to find favour and ready sale, had to reflect the feelings, opinions, and wishes, the likings and the hates, the prejudices and the passions of the operatives whose only poetry they constitute. These are their lyrics, their odes, their poems, their satires, their sonnets, and their songs all in one. What then was the character of these half literary half oral element which was ever operating on the feelings of the large masses of the least educated portion of our community?[1]

The broadsides in this anthology give some indication of the character of literature preferred by northern operatives during the years 1750-1880. As the 'only poetry' of the people the reader will find a surprising richness, variety and beauty, reflecting the feelings, desires and attitudes of working people in the midst of the great changes brought by industrialisation. Many of these broadsides are not specifically northern in origin, but were known throughout England; or as popular London songs, they were stolen by northern printers. But, the collection emphasises northern work, leisure and speech. Coal mining, weaving, wakes' festivals, and other specifically northern occupations and customs are all included, in addition to the more general themes of courting, love, sport and, of course, murder and passion.

The broadside was the most widespread form of written literature from the beginning of printing. It was the chief reading matter of the poor, with the price rarely varying over three and a half centuries of publication—a penny or halfpenny. (In the sixteenth and seventeenth centuries the very poor clubbed together to buy a sheet on the latest event, murder or supernatural occurrence). Technically a broadside is a sheet of rough quality paper with writing on one side in either prose or poetry; a boardsheet contains print on both sides. Most broadsides were verse ballads or narratives of romance, chivalry, murder or current events, though advertisements, short tales, or last dying speeches were also sold, in combination with verse or separately. From their beginning sellers were notorious for either falsifying or claiming to have new information when selling a reprint. These wares were called 'catch-pennies' or 'cocks'. The chaunter's patter usually included a reference to 'a curate in the vicinity' or 'lovers from a nearby street', giving sufficient detail to entice listeners into believing he knew something unusual about their immediate neighbourhood. Almost all broadsides had a woodcut supposedly illustrating the reading matter, but in fact chosen to attract potential buyers, with little attempt to fit the verses. Many printers bought old woodcuts from their wealthier peers and used them until they broke or wore out. An excellent likeness of Sir Francis Bacon is said to have adorned a seventeenth century tale or murder and repentence.

Sixteenth and seventeenth century ballads had headlines printed in an old fashioned Gothic type and so are called 'Black letter.' 'White letter,' or Roman type, broadsides gradually replaced them in the late seventeenth and early eighteenth century. Until recently almost all scholarship has centered on the older boardsides; many of these are our only printed version of traditional folk songs or of important political quarrels. Black letter ballads included musical notation, which could be totally jumbled, but did indicate the popularity of contemporary tunes. The frank sensuality and strong political commentary of many Black letter ballads led church men to seek government interference to halt their publication; they were successful in insuring the registration of ballads, but not their irradication. The Puritans were even more zealous in persecuting sellers; during the years 1649-59 all itinerant ballads singers were subject to arrest and the trade went underground. After the Restoration sales recommenced with no loss of popularity. Indeed, the Society for Promoting Christian Knowledge, founded in the late seventeenth century, used the disreputable broadside as a cheap and attractive way to disseminate its propaganda.[2]

The other popular form of publishing cheap literature was chap-books—a quarto sheet, or sometimes several sheets, folded to make eight or more pages; the buyer cut the pages and fastened them together with a pin. Chapbooks were preeminantly the reading material of the poor in the eighteenth century; their widespread use laid the foundations of mass literacy. Traditional tales such as Mother Goose, Cock Robin, and Guy of Warwick, still told to English speaking children, were first available to the general public in chapbooks. Small song books, or 'garlands' selling for three pence were particularly popular around Newcastle. Unlike chapbooks, they were always eight pages and never included prose narratives. There was no musical notation, but such comments as 'To a traditional air' or 'To the tune of Barbara Allen' were occasionally appended. Many garlands were sold to the young men of northern towns who wished to keep up with the latest hits sung at the theatres and supper clubs, though the best known traditional songs were also included.

White letter broadsides were smaller than Black letter and were frequently double columned. Slips could then be cut in half and sold at bargain rates. The price and date were never printed on the sheet so the chaunter could charge whatever the traffic would bear, and could always claim to be selling the latest item on the market. Woodcuts were often quite elaborate in the eighteenth century, as broadside No. 1 shows. The paper used was a cheap grey-blue stock until new methods of paper-making became widespread, and competition from Catnach, the largest London printer, brought in a thin white paper. Gradually standards of printing fell under the pressures of mass production. Peculiarities of type abound in all boardsides, but they seem more common in the nineteenth century. Printers used Italic letters when they ran out of Roman; various lower case letters were substituted for each other, such as 'b,' 'p,' 'q,' and 'd'. The results were rarely proof-read, leading to further errors.

By the beginning of the nineteenth century hundreds of printers sold broadsides (75 in London alone), achieving record sales throughout the country. H. Such, the London printer, had over 5,000 titles available for wholesale purchase. Catnach's broadsides on the murders of Rush and on the Mannings each sold two and a half million copies.[3] It was the boast of sellers everywhere that they could beat a newspaper any day in publishing the last words of a murderer at his hanging—they simply printed their version before the event. The only rivals in circulation were the Religious Tract Society, founded in 1799, and a reactivated S.P.C.K. In the year 1820, 700,000 tracts were published by the S.P.C.K. Like Catnach it found executions a good site for disseminating its broadsides; at one 42,575 were distributed; at another 40,850.[4] Since most of its tracts were given away, usually by the benevolent or fearful upper classes, it is difficult to estimate how many were actually read by the recipients. Whatever their purpose broadsides—and all cheap printed matter—were a large and growing business in the early years of the nineteenth century.

After 1850 broadsides gradually declined in popularity, to be replaced by the yellow press and cheap serial novels. Although jugglers, acrobats and the like continued their street entertainments into the twentieth century, the ballad singer and seller was a rarity by the time Leary came to explore street literature. Indeed, he found that most sellers used broadsides as a front while dealing primarily in pornography and contraceptives. Accurate news could be found in cheap newspapers, and other forms of entertainment offered more variety than the chaunter. Higher standards of literacy meant a greater demand for accuracy and reliability in all forms of reading matter. Working people everywhere came to prefer the warmth and comfort of a singing hall where they could hear, and buy, a copy of the latest popular song. Sellers had always traded on their novelty and modernity; when they could offer neither, their demise was inevitable.

BROADSIDE PRINTERS, WRITERS AND SELLERS

As a commercial venture broadsides sold well for the enterprising man who combined national favourites with local themes; profit was the main aim. The three largest printers in the north were John Harkness of Preston, John Swindells of Manchester and John Marshall of Newcastle (not to be confused with the Religious Tract publisher of the same name). Unfortunately we know little about these men's careers, and even less about their sales figures and profits. They probably compare closely, however, with Jemmy Catnach, except in the size of their business. Catnach is said to have earned £500 on the sales for Rush's murder alone, and up to £10,000 in his career (1814-41).[5] Sales in the north for a popular ballad such as "The Devil's in the Girl" (No. 40) were probably between 30,000 and 50,000 copies over a period of many years (ballads on general subjects could be sold over and over, unlike those on a particular murder or current event). Earnings for the most prolific publishers probably ran in the region of £100 annually, including other printing jobs.

There was always a considerable exchange of songs between northern and London printers. Indeed, in the 1860's and 70's several of Edwin Waugh's Lancashire dialect songs appear as anonymous works published by London firms, despite being under copyright (see No. 41). John Harkness reprinted many of Catnach's most popular works, in addition to his own repertoire of local songs. He appears to have begun printing around 1838 and continued until 1875-80. His numbered broadsides go as high as 1,200, though no complete collection exists. In addition to broadsides, he sold penny books, chapbooks, Christmas carols, directories, and briefly in 1874, he printed and published 'The Preston Illustrated Times.' He specialized in ballads on a subject—love, patriotism, local events and contemporary scenes, rather than murders and catchpennies. His career spans the heyday and decline of broadsides. At his death his vast collection of blocks, print and stock were taken to Blackburn and sold for waste material.[6]

Far less is known about John Swindells or John Marshall. Swindells inherited his business from his father in 1796 and continued until 1846 at Hanging Bridge and Old Churchyard, in one of the oldest districts of Manchester. He was chiefly known as a printer of broadsides and chapbooks, including "Cock Robin" and "Jenny Wren." He also sold a popular history of England in serial form. Since his wife continued the business after his death the exact date of its end is unclear.[7] Marshall, after a series of fires, went bankrupt in 1831; he was a book-seller, stationer and printer with offices in Gateshead from 1801 to 1810, and then he moved to Newcastle. The advertisement for the auction of his effects included 6,000 volumes from his circulating library and 'upwards of 300 superior Wood-Cuts, of great Beauty and Variety, by the celebrated Mr. Bewick.'[8] In addition to publishing garlands, broadsides and chapbooks, he printed some of the earliest trade union pamphlets for the miners' union of 1825 and 1826. No. 20 is an example of his work for the miners' union in 1831.

In spite of immense sales, few northern publishers relied entirely on broadsides for their income. Distribution was dependent upon itinerant hawkers, and could be unreliable outside the immediate city of publication, despite the frequent advertisements on boardsides notifying salesmen, 'Travellers supplied and Country Orders punctually attended to.' Most local printers, however, did find it profitable to print broadsides as a sideline, at the request of either a local song writer, or an individual or group seeking publicity. For example, John Procter of Hartlepool was the only printer in the town for several years and soon had a wide reputation for cheap and conscientious work. He printed everything a small industrial town might need—advertisements, playbills, posters, calling cards, account forms, cheques, and on occasion broadsides. During the 1844 Durham and Northumberland coal mining strike he printed "A New Song" (No. 25) for William Armstrong, manager of the Wingate Grange Colliery. Armstrong sent a copy of the poem to Procter with a warning against revealing the source of the work. Within twenty-four hours the poem was published as the true voice of a disillusioned pitman. Procter never revealed the truth, though he kept Armstrong's letter with the note "My oath of secrecy shall not be broken."[9] Most political poems did not have such a clandestine history, though many times a printer was called upon not to reveal the source of a political attack or personal threat he had printed.

Broadside writers and singers can be divided into two groups: those who wrote or sang as an occupation and those who did so only for particular occasions. Full time writers of broadsides earned a precarious living churning out rhymed verse on whatever subject seemed popular at the moment. Catnach and other large London publishers kept individuals sitting by their printing presses to write about an event as soon as the news was received. These men were commonly paid a shilling a song, regardless of future sales. Mayhew estimated their number to be only six in London and their weekly earnings to average ten shillings, a pittance in comparison with publishers' earnings.[10] While London writers did not usually hawk their own works, northern writers did.

They built up a round of public houses and friendly neighbourhoods where they sang and sold their works. In many cases they became spokesmen for the working men of a particular trade and were expected to compose songs during strikes, hard times and festivals. In return they were kept supplied with beer and other necessities. The writer-singer was an essential member of many northern industrial communities in the later eighteenth and early nineteenth centuries.

Part time writers wrote broadside songs or prose for a particular cause. They felt strongly committed to a trade union strike (see Nos. 24, 26 and 27), temperance (see No. 47) or religion (see No. 28). These writers neither expected nor received payment for their works, beyond the respect of their friends and perhaps a round of free beer. On occasion, however, necessity drove an unemployed operative or miner to write and sell his own songs to buy bread for his family. This was only done under particularly severe distress and was considered degrading for a skilled worker. During the Lancashire Cotton Famine, 1861-65, working men and their families could be seen on the streets of all the cotton-producing cities singing hyms and selling broadsides, old clothes and tinker's goods. Not surprisingly, broadside sellers in woodcuts are often elderly men and women, or women with young children—individuals who could not earn their living in a more established way.

Broadsides written for purposes other than pure entertainment have been neg-lected, yet they are just as much a part of the popular literature of the times as anything produced by Harkness, Catnach or Swindells. As works written for and by working men and women under the stress of a momentous occasion, or a deeply held belief, they may be considered more authentic voices of working class sentiment and belief than the products of professional ballad writers. The sale of trade union, temperance and religious broadsides was almost exclusively the province of volunteers anxious to spread the word about their cause and to raise money. Trade unions needed to convince others of the justness of their position and to counter the information spread by such men as Armstrong with his "New Song." Because they were cheap, popular, and easy to distribute, broadsides became the principal form of propaganda in coal mining areas during a strike. In the early stages of the temperance movement the sale of broadsides helped to pay an itinerant speaker's expenses; the converted had a duty to buy and sell his works. In the 1860's and '70's the Band of Hope was zealous in distributing broad-side songs to children describing the evils of drink, and the value of literacy combined with teetotal principles. Frequently broadsides were given away at church picnics in commemoration of the event. George Hanby, known as 'Peter Pledge,' for his advocacy of temperance, titled one of his pieces, "Verses on the Temperance and Sunday School Tea Meeting, held on the 11th of November, 1864, in Miss Pilkington's Reading Room, Newmillerdam, near Wakefield, convened for the purposes of presenting a testimonial to Mr. William Gates of Rotherham, late of Barnsley, for his unwearied zeal in the Church Sunday School at Walton."

The full time sellers considered themselves members of a skilled craft, above costermongers and other street vendors; they were skilled performers who could sing and entertain. Their income, however, was as precarious as that of all street sellers. It varied markedly with the weather (rain or snow emptied the streets) and the topicality of the broadsides offered (a murder could be discussed only so long and then was stale news). Most chaunters relied on a few houses where they knew they could receive donations, either to leave the neighbourhood or because a wealthy gentleman collected broadsides. Mayhew calculated that chaunters who sang, about two hundred in London in 1851, averaged three shillings a day, while other broadside sellers earned 7/6 to 10/6 per week.[11] Probably few northern sellers earned more than ten shillings a week except when they offered a 'new' account of a recent murder or a popular attack on a local politician.

The major impetus for buying a broadside among most working people was the chaunter's skillful singing and acting. According to all accounts a chaunter, as the name would indicate, sang in a monotonous flat twang, perhaps to conserve his voice or to be heard above the other street noises. He often began with a spoken patter, directed towards the audience gathering around, including some local gossip and commentary, while recommending the purchase of the new song about to be rendered. He would then launch into selected verses, calling upon the audience to join in the choruses, pausing to make sales, while keeping an eye out for the police or possible trouble-makers. The conclusion of the tale was usually left off in order to encourage buying the broadside. Those who performed in pubs were dependent upon the largess of the publican, but they had their faithful clientele and earned a smaller but possibly steadier living. Their singing style was similar to outdoor chaunters, but with more emphasis on group singing and songs about the pleasures of drink. Convivial entertainment made the pub more attractive—an important side-effect for the publican.

In the larger cities broadside sellers specialized in both their selling methods and material. A 'running patterer' worked with other persons, who ran about shouting out the latest news or catch phrases such as 'Horrible,' 'Frightening', 'Recent Event.' They would then, amidst the clamour they had started, point to the seller, who would sell as many copies as he could without revealing the contents. These broadsides were frequently cocks; the Houses of Parliament burnt down several times for the benefit of these salesmen. Running patterers could not work the same neighbourhood frequently lest their tricks become well known. In rural areas 'death-hunters' created quite a stir. These sellers walked from village to village selling last dying speeches and execution scenes. They carried a long pole with a canvas suspended between cross-bars. On one side was a vivid scene of the murder, and on the other that of the execution. The broadsides they sold, of course, purported to carry an authentic picture of the villain, who invariably confessed his guilt and begged pardon of man and God just before his death.

It is difficult to calculate how frequently or persistently chaunters were persecuted for their sales, or noise or as general nuisances in the late eighteenth and nineteenth century. Their reputation for chicanery and dishonesty probably contributed to public criticism of them. As early as 1819 the residents of Oldham Street, Manchester, present-ed the following petition to the magistrates:

> We the undersigned inhabitants of Oldham Street, Manchester, respectively [sic] present this memorial to your worship;—That we are everyday (except Sundays) troubled with the pestilent and grievous nuisance of profane and debauched ballad singing, by men and women, to the corrupting of the minds and morals of the public in general, and our children and servants in particular. We therefore most humbly request, that you will use the power committed to you, in removing this evil immediately; and we will ever acknowledge of the benefit.[12]

According to Leary the respectful and respectable inhabitants were successful in their petition, and from that time Manchester's police worked to eradicate such public nuisances as were drawn to their attention. It is easy for us to romanticise the old chaunters, but this letter is a reminder that nineteenth century cities were as noisy as our modern cities with motorised traffic.

Although we know almost nothing about northern publishers, we are fortunate in having the life stories and many personal anecdotes about several popular local ballad writers and singers. Most provincial singers turned to chaunting either from a love of freedom or because of a physical disability. In coal mining towns singers were almost all ex-miners injured in a pit accident. Much of the verse written by these eccentrics that survives is heavily satiric and pointed directly at a particular issue of the day, whereas the ballads they might buy from a local printer were usually reprints of popular songs with little conscious local identity (unconscious variations crept in when a local typesetter altered words to fit his own dialect). By selling a mixture of local material, love ballads and popular London songs a chaunter could appeal to the widest possible audience.

One of the most colorful ballad writers and performers of the early days of industrialism was Joseph Mather (1737-1804) from Sheffield. He sold his songs riding through town sitting backwards on a donkey, from which he would sing, cajole and sell. On one rainy day he rode straight into his favourite public house. He attended all the fairs and races, singing and hawking with great sucess, if memories of the time are to be trusted. His influence among the cutlers and other artisans attached to the cutlery trade was great. They particularly delighted in "W————'s Thirteens," an attack on the Master-Cutler Watkinson, who tried to enforce thirteen knives to the dozen when paying workmen in the 1780's (see No. 4). For years afterwards any master-cutler quaked when he heard the words, though it is recorded that one apprentice was jailed for humming the tune under his breath.[13] Mather's violence and exaggerated threats were condemned by later Sheffield singers, but he came from a long tradition of political attack and song writing that called for such language, combined with allusions to Biblical stories and God's justice to be wrought against those who mistreated working men.

Bradford's eccentric chaunter was Reuben Holder (1719-?). He was a licensed hawker who had started life as a trapper boy at five years, later became a brickmaker, and finally a seller of fish and poetry. He was a strong teetotaller before the temperance movement began and wrote many poems against drink. Holder entered eagerly into the issues of his day, and wrote appropriate verses for all the important events in Bradford. He supported Oastler's factory movement, but attacked the local Owenites as godless and "poor silly men . . . those cowards and shufflers" for their refusal to debate with the Rev. Joseph Barker (see No. 17). One of his most popular broadsides was "The New Starvation Law Examined—on the new British Bastiles" (see No. 16). The working men of Yorkshire, as those in other parts of England, hated the new Poor Law of 1834, which enforced the separation of married couples in the workhouse, and brought degradation and humility to those who had spent a lifetime earning their living respectably. Like so many early criticisms of the factory system, Holder's prime attack was against regimentation in the 'Bastilles'—orders down to the minutest details were issued to the workhouse men and women on how they should behave, giving them no alternative to prison-like conditions except starvation. When Holder was not entertaining the public with his popular opinions he composed such items as "Verses on the Coronation," and "Verses on the Christening of the Prince of Wales," all exhibiting widespread loyalty among the residents of Bradford to the young Queen and her growing family.

Town commentators such as Mather and Holder were common until the middle of the nineteenth century (and to this day men can be found in village pubs, willing to sing satiric verse for a drink). But, increasingly the penny reader and the music hall entertainer replaced the broadside chaunter. The more regulated life of the later part of the century meant less overt violence, and also less idiosyncratic behaviour. The greater demands made by a better educated working class audience, combined with greater opportunities for high wages, led to the 'professionalisation' of entertainment. An established dialect reader could earn thirty shillings for an evening's entertainment, while music hall singers, performing twice nightly, often earned £2 and £3 for an evening in the 1860's, and by the 1890's as high as £20 and £30. Talented young singers eagerly embraced the hard discipline of touring the provinces on one-night stands for such rewards—and the possibility of reaching London's famed halls. For many years chaunters and music hall singers existed side by side, borrowing songs and patter from each other. The most important carry-over from the older, simpler form of entertainment was the continuation of audience participation. Artistes expected their audience to sing the chorus, to roar out their approval (or disapproval) and to buy their songs with the same vigour audiences had greeted travelling theatrical performers and ballad chaunters. Chaunters, who were steadily losing ground to the halls, frequently plagarized or openly stole popular music hall songs, even identifying the local singer in some cases on the broadside itself (see No. 46), hoping thereby to compete with the singer and his more sedate methods of selling.

The rich singing tradition of the north-east had long produced famous local singers and actors who celebrated the wonders of Tyneside in song. One of the most beloved music hall artistes who came out of this tradition was Ned Corvan (1830-65). He was briefly apprenticed to a sailmaker, but left work to join Billy Purvis's theatre company. He was very popular, but Purvis kept him in bit parts lest he upstage his own comic art. In 1850 when the opportunity came to be the 'local singer' at a new concert hall in Newcastle, Corvan left acting permanently. His early training, however, led him to emphasise the dramatic routine accompanying a song more than the song itself. One speciality of his was drawing pictures while he talked and sang; his most popular caricature was his old master. A story is told of how one night Corvan started his sketch when a voice cried out 'Myek us a cuddy [ass], Ned,' Corvan immediately replied, 'All reet, stand up,' bringing the house down, and winning more loyal fans.[14]

Corvan brought an unfailing sympathy for working people to his songs. He was particularly good at portraying the plight of a widow left with many children. (His own father had died at five, and he grew up without any formal education.) A favourite song of the time, and still appropriate today, was "The Toon Improvement Bill, or ne pleyce noo te play" (No. 32). Urban renewal then as now did not take into consideration the needs of children when a profit might be made from an 'improvement,' in this case a new railway station. Corvan's combination of patter and song was also characteristic of the newer, more sophisticated mode of presenting songs—much depended upon interpretation, gesture and intonation. In "The Toon Improvement Bill" comic gestures or grimaces could undercut and demean the plight of the narrator, who had to combine sympathy with humour.

The north-east's most famous music hall entertainer was Joe Wilson (1841-75). According to his autobiography, 'Me fether was a joiner an' cabinet myeker, an' me muther a straw bonnit myeker,—an byeth natives o' the "canny aud toon o' Newcassil."' He was apprenticed to a printer at the age of fourteen, and through his kindness, published a chapbook of his songs at seventeen. By 21 Wilson had his own small shop, but like Corvan, he inherited tuberculosis and did not have the stamina to run a business. He then took up the equally arduous career of music hall artiste, where he achieved rapid success. He disliked travelling, and tried at various times to run a public house, a temperance hotel, and finally edited an almanac modelled after Cruikshank's *Comic Almanack*. While successful enough in all these ventures, the greater rewards of entertaining brought him back into the music hall circuit until his premature death. A very modest man, Wilson always insisted, when his works were praised throughout England, 'I don't call myself a poet, I call myself a song-writer.'[15]

Like Corvan, Wilson was interested in the affairs of working people, but he concentrated more on the attitudes of working men involved in the trade unions gathering strength through the 1860's and 70's. In 1871 he wrote a number of strike songs for the engineers at Armstrong's factory during their drive for a nine hour working day (see Nos. 34 and 35). Wilson was more interested in the emotional responses of a working man and his family to the strike than the political or legal issues involved. Conciliation and hope marked all of his songs; though on occasion he could be sardonic, he preferred to emphasise the gentler feelings of his characters, and to appeal to the audience's emotions.

The lives of all of these men, and many more like them, were precarious in every way—working class entertainment throughout the period was economically marginal. Extra money for songs came on an impulse or in good times or from the young. Yet these singers managed to survive and to remain free from the discipline of ordinary labour; while remaining a part of the working people, they were free agents, ready to comment on, criticise, and enjoy the life around them. The changes wrought by nearly a century of industrialisation are obvious—the harsh curses of Mather contrast sharply with the gentle humour of Wilson's songs. Yet each is equally a spokesman for working men and women, and each is representative of the richness and strengths of the 'half literary half oral element' of entertainment available on the streets, in the pubs and in the halls of England's northern towns during the long years of the industrial revolution.

THE SUBJECT MATTER OF INDUSTRIAL BROADSIDES

Charles Hindley, the most famous nineteenth century collector, divided the subject matter of broadsides into four categories: (1) Catchpennies and street drolleries. This included a wide variety of material, almost all purporting to be about actual events; the only common denominator was the comic treatment of the subject. (2) Royalty and politics, (3) 'Gallows' literature—last dying confessions, descriptions of murders, hangings and the like, and (4) Ballads on a subject. This broad category included almost everything touching on current events or well known persons that was not directly political.[16] Hindley did not classify the broadside propaganda printed by trade unions, temperance societies and religious groups because he appears not to have considered their material entertainment (although clearly much of it was written both to amuse and to educate). Hindley's categories are helpful when examining the vast numbers of extant broadsides, but they do not help us to see how industrial broadsides differed from or were similar to their predecessors. Subject matter became more varied, reflecting the new inventions, educational opportunities, and concern with current events. In the north we find a greater emphasis on the impact of such industrial changes as factory work, railways, and the employment of women in industry, whereas foreign affairs, royalty and such events as the Great Exhibition appear less frequently than in London broadsides. A far more important change, however, was in the treatment of traditional subject matter. Love, murder and politics were still the major topics of broadsides, but they showed a new realism and concern for the everyday life of the common man or woman. While industrial ballads lack the harsh beauty and emotional power of traditional folk songs, they are as worthy of study as the earlier works—no better source can be found for an understanding of the everyday lives, hopes and fears of the industrial worker.

The most obvious change in industrial broadsides was the new emphasis on realism; although various events might seem improbable, they were always possible. The differences between the newer broadsides and the older can be seen by comparing "The Honour of a London Prentice" (No. 1) and "The Sheffield Apprentice" (No. 2). "The London Prentice" dates from the reign of Queen Elizabeth, though this particular copy is a reprint from the early eighteenth century. It is a Renaissance version of the medieval quest, whereby the knight's moral courage is tested through physically daunting adventures. God's miraculous intervention saves the 'prentice from being devoured by the lions, but since this is a sixteenth century poem, a rational explanation is also given: they are "faint for Food" and therefore less able to gobble him up. In contrast, the Sheffield apprentice (No. 2 is a London reprint of this immensely popular tale) undergoes a very probable adventure. The characters, setting and emotions are stereotyped but realistic, and certainly familiar to eighteenth century readers. (Modern readers may remember that Joseph Andrews' mistress threatened him in a similar manner when he refused her advances). The 'prentice's faithful love for his pretty Polly is another symptom of changing values; though class lines might be crossed by true lovers, the choice to do so had to be mutual. The realistic base of "The Sheffield Apprentice" is, nevertheless, combined with many traditional folk elements; for example, there is a mysterious lady, a trip to a foreign country and a vow of revenge, with the gold ring as a talisman. What has changed is not so much the basic ingredients of a love story, but the treatment of them. The events are recorded from the point of view of the common man as he himself might undergo them, not as he might if he were elevated to a form of knighthood.

While magic and miracles were no longer a part of broadside tales, love ballads remained the most popular subject matter. Perhaps it was because women and young men were the primary buyers of broadsides that love, courting and sex were such favourite topics. Whatever the reason, no chaunter could be without a full array of sad ballads of love betrayed, humorous accounts of courting and a few sly tales of marriage or sex. Ballad writers, and buyers, were not held back by Victorian conventions in regard to sexual matters—woman enjoyed sex as much as men, and were often far more demanding (See "The Devil's in the Girl," No. 40). Not every woman was chaste, modest and limp; aggressive women, indeed, are the norm in broadsides. "Never Maids Wed An Old Man (No. 49) is typical of the robust honesty of nineteenth century broadsides. Equally comic, of course, was the confused young man from the country; "Slap-up Lodgings" (No. 39) is an exaggeration of what many country bumpkins may have felt. Almost no broadsides survive which can be called pornographic or obscene; without the inhibitions of their betters, working people could be more open and cheerful about sex, even though they might seem casual or cruel at times.

Eating, playing and agricultural work have long been metaphors for sexual intercourse. Many broadsides dating from before the Industrial Revolution, but reprinted well into the nineteenth century, tell of the sower sowing his seed, leaving the woman to reap a 'bonny bairn.' The majority of these ballads seem obvious, even silly, to the more sophisticated reader, but an excellent exception is "The Mower", (No. 5), describing a young man's sexual impotence with delicacy and candour—a combination rare enough in any age or literature. "The New Bury Loom" (No. 7), first published around 1800, is a good example of an early industrial ballad about sex based on the technical terms involved in weaving. While very similar to the earlier agricultural ballads, it shows a new relish in the craft of weaving. The vocabulary is an amusing combination of weaving terms and overtly sexual images, such as 'breast beam,' 'down on her warp' and 'nickety nack,' which is not only onomatopoeic for the motion of the loom, but also was slang for the female sexual organs. The joiner is the traditional roving rake and a skilled technician, needed to square, or fix, the new Dobbie looms (similar to Jacquard looms, they permitted the weaving of elaborate patterns, but needed frequent attention).

Early in the nineteenth century broadside writers began using the factory, coal mine or other industrial occupations as background for a love story. In many cases this was simply an old tale altered to fit the new conditions. The prince marrying the chaste peasant maid became the rich stranger marrying the factory girl in "The Fortunate Factory Girl" (No. 11). In the realistic "Sam Shuttle and Betty Reedhook" (No. 13) the factory is little more than a backdrop for her courtship by Tom Cut-looker, in contrast to "The New Bury Loom" where the working of the loom defines both the weaver and the joiner. These love stories must have appealed most to those many operatives, men and women, who found their lives uneventful and unnoticed. Based on familiar situations and details, they enabled individuals to identify with the hero or heroine and to escape to love or adventure, finding there the satisfaction missing from their personal lives.

While not every factory girl expected to meet a rich stranger on her way to work, each could anticipate courtship and marriage. Once again broadsides reflect prevailing attitudes towards marriage and its demands on both men and women. The majority of writers took an ironic and humorous view of the institution, though the influence of Queen Victoria can be seen in the latter half of the nineteenth century, when the family hearth became an idealized haven for all working men. The very good humour of "My Wife's First Baby" (No. 43) is characteristic of the treatment of marriage and its inevitable pitfalls, although there were also bitter commentaries on shrewishness, drunkenness and physical abuse. A very popular topic was the difficulty of raising a family on an inadequate wage: expenses were listed under such titles as "Fifteen shillings a week" (No. 44), or eighteen, or even eight. While love ballads still ended 'happily ever after,' there were plenty of accounts of marriage to forewarn romantic buyers.

Love ballads were pleasant fantasies that might come true, but hard times broke into such dreams all too often. While industrialisation brought an improved standard of living for some, it also brought increased social and economic pressures of every sort. A repeated theme in broadsides of the time was the possible consolations of marriage and family love in the face of unemployment, emigration and inexplicable economic crises. But, other more active alternatives were also sought, which are reflected in broadsides—political protest, such as the Ten Hours Movement (No. 18), trade unionism, such as the Miners' Association of Great Britain and Ireland (No. 24), and religion, such as Primitive Methodism (No. 28). Organisations published inumerable protest ballads, describing in pathetic verses the plight of factory children or miners or drunkards. The reader was expected to feel pity and guilt, and to change his ways. Other protest songs were aimed at the converted—hymns, rallying chants, and comic dialogues were written to encourage flagging spirits. Many of these broadsides were directly reflective of working class culture and values. For example, the elegy for Mr. Thomas Briggs (No. 19) was written in memory of a Chartist; the piece is not directly political, but comes out of the heartfelt friendship derived from shared political goals and activities.

One Lancashire protest poem has lasted until our own day—the consolatory ballad "Jone o' Grinfilt." The original version (No. 8) was written during a depression in the 1790's by Joseph Lees, a schoolmaster from near Oldham.[17] It was immediately a best seller; within a few years a dozen imitations circulated throughout the north (Nos. 9 and 10 are but two examples). Broadside writers came to use John Greenfield as the name of a Lancashire adventurer. The finest version was "Jone o' Grinfilt, Jr." (No. 9), written around 1819 during a time of severe economic and social repression. (The broadside printed here is from the 1860's, when it was revived by the unemployed cotton operatives suffering from the American Civil War and the blockade of southern cotton supplies; note the change to Queen in the last stanza). Margaret's threat to visit the king became proverbial during hard times in Lancashire. The poem is a remarkable combination of consolation and protest. The weaver has no desire to overturn society, but he will not tolerate injustice. He attacks those in power—the church parson, the putter-out, the shop-keeper and the house owner—but accepts economic instability. Self-respect, and a willingness to fight for it, is the basis of the poem; revolutionary change is not seen as an alternative.

Self-respect was the basis of many protest ballads. Not all, however, were as resigned as "Jone." One of the most famous political events of the time was Peterloo; many broadsides were published condemning it—and a few in its defence. On 16 August 1819 some 60,000 working people gathered at St. Peter's Fields in Manchester to hear the famous radical orator Henry Hunt. The event was widely advertised as a peaceful demonstration, but the frightened magistrates called up the local yeomanry and the Hussars. Hunt was arrested just as he began speaking; at the same time the cavalry charged into the densely packed crowds, slashing with their swords. Eleven were killed and some four hundred injured. Outraged at this breach in public freedom, spokesmen from Parliament down to the meanest broadside writer spoke out against the hasty actions of the government. Harkness's broadside "Peterloo" (No. 5) is most characteristic of the attitudes of Lancashire's working class: echoing Tom Paine, the anonymous author calls for "fair freedom's sons" to rise in defence of their unalienable rights.

The songs written immediately after Peterloo were all similar in their hatred of the government; they were immediate reactions to a particular event, rather than a reasoned defence of the Radicals' position. A much more difficult task was forging a union that would resist tyranny over many months, even years. During the early years of the nineteenth century Northumberland and County Durham were centres for trade union organizing amongst colliers, sailors and keelmen. The broadsides written by these unions concern themselves with gaining public good will and convincing other workers to remain loyal to the union. The most violent attack was not against the owners but against blacklegs. "First Drest Man of Seghill or the Pitman's Reward for Betraying his Brethren" (No. 20) was written just before the first successful colliery strike of Northumberland and County Durham. The pitmen had refused to sign the annual bond, which fell due 5 April 1831, until their demands were met; during the weeks immediately preceding and after that date roving bands of colliers waylaid individuals suspected of sympathising with the coal owners and roughed them up. Summary justice of this sort outraged the general public and laid the foundation for future troubles. But by the middle of June the owners capitulated to the union's demands; payment by script and Tommy shops were stopped and the labour of boys was limited to twelve hours. A massive celebration was held in August on Bolden Fell, between Gateshead and Sunderland. "The Pitmen's Agreement" (No. 21) was one of many broadsides written for the occasion; the emphasis is on the justice of the pitmen's demands—a theme repeated throughout the nineteenth century by all working men and women during their fight for better economic and social conditions.[18]

Flushed with victory, the union made further demands in the spring of 1832 when the bond once again fell due. This time the owners had stockpiled coal, and were determined to stand united against the union—and to destroy it. "Candy-men" were hired to evict strikers from the company-owned housing. Once again the two counties were in turmoil. Just when it was clear the union would collapse an event occurred which shocked both sides: Nicholas Fairles, magistrate for County Durham, was attacked by two drunken pitmen, William Jobling and Ralph Anderson. He lived on ten days and was able to identify his assailants. Anderson managed to escape, some say to America, in spite of the large reward offered for his capture. Jobling was apprehended and sentenced to death by public hanging and gibbeting. Boardside No. 15 describes the event in graphic detail. Although there seems to be no doubt that Jobling was guilty, public opinion was inflamed by the discrepancy between his sentence and the six months imprisonment given to a policeman found guilty of killing a pitman. Despite heavy penalties, one night Jobling's body was stolen from the gibbet and never recovered. His memory has survived in local legends; for years pitmen threatened children with his ghost if they refused to go to bed promptly.[19]

The fight to establish a permanent pitmen's union took the better half of the century—and the bitterness and violence of the struggle is reflected in the broadsides written by both sides. Conditions for seamen, engineers and other workers were often just as grim, and their struggles are mirrored in many broadsides (See Nos. 29, 34 and 35).

The exhortations to duty and action which characterised so many industrial ballads should not be our final view of northern broadsides. Rather, the infinite amount of humour, laughter and parody should remind us of the happier side of life for those who bought and read broadsides. The gulling of southerners or the follies of courting couples were just as much a part of industrial traditions as the protest ballads. The cheap day return and Sunday sea excursion trip provided new topics for larking. Each area of the north had its particular customs—How many commuters into Newcastle remember that the Town Moor was the scene of numerous pitmen's rallies, political meetings and foot races (see No. 48)? The last Preston Guild was in 1921, but every twenty years throughout the nineteenth century the event was the largest holiday in

Lancashire (see No. 49), bringing together all the trade unions, factories, religious organisations and other groups, who marched with their respective banners, uniforms and songs. Hawkers of broadsides did a thriving business on such days, and other special occasions, such as horse races, fairs, and public hangings.

The broadsides of the late nineteenth century do not differ markedly from earlier pieces, except perhaps in exhibiting a greater acceptance of industrial conditions, and greater confidence in the power of working people to control these conditions. "The Greet Strike" (No. 34), for example, combines humour, political comment and social observation. Although 'Improvemints cum but slowly roond,' Wilson and his readers had seen sufficient changes in their lifetime to struggle for a better future. "Owdham Street at Dinner Time" is an amusing description of the many changes to be seen in the factory districts. Confident of their position in society, the workers rejoiced in the wealth which they helped to create. Local pride went hand in hand with local prosperity and a sense of individual worth.

In recent years efforts have been made in Wigan, Newcastle and Manchester to revive the selling of broadsides and the writing of occasional verse. On the whole these works have been well received at folk song clubs, but have not extended beyond them. Conditions have changed—we can buy broadsides nowadays as commemorative of specific events, just as our ancestors did, but we no longer trust the printed word as the whole truth, nor are we particularly impressed with a performer singing on a street corner. While valuing these flimsy papers as curious documents of the past, we should not mourn the passing of conditions which made the purchase—and reading—of a broadside an intellectual effort. The works that follow should be enjoyed as they were by earlier readers—as reminders of the richness and variety of human experience, the need for understanding in times of stress and for courage and humour in the face of emotional fears or political oppression.

FOOTNOTES

1. Fred Leary, manuscript collection, n. d. [1893], Manchester Central Reference Library.

2. The fullest description of the Black-letter ballad is Hyder Rollins, "The Black-Letter Broadside Ballad," *PMLA*, XXXIV (1919), 258-339.

3. Charles Hindley, *History of the Catnach Press* (London, 1887), p. 92.

4. R. K. Webb, *The British Working Class Reader* (London, 1955), pp. 27-57.

5. Charles Hindley, *The Life and Times of James Catnach* (London, 1887), p. 142, and Henry Mayhew, *London Labour and the London Poor* (London, 1861), I, 220.

6. J. H. Spencer, "A Preston Chap Book and its Printer," *Preston Herald*, 2 January 1948.

7. "John Swindells, Printer," *Manchester City News Notes and Queries*, V (19 December 1883), 178-179.

8. Quoted from Frances M. Thomson, *Newcastle Chapbooks in Newcastle upon Tyne University Library* (Newcastle, 1969), p. 12.

9. I am indebted to Robert Wood of Hartlepool for permitting me to examine the papers of John Procter. The handwritten copy of "A New Song" and Armstrong's letter were placed on Procter's spike file for 1844.

10. Mayhew, I, 178-280.

11. Mayhew, I, 306-309.

12. Quoted by Leary, manuscript notes, from *Imperial Magazine*, May, 1819.

13. John Wilson, "Memoir of Mather," *The Songs of Joseph Mather*, ed. John Wilson (Sheffield, 1862), pp. vii-xxiv.

14. *Allan's Tyneside Songs*, eds. T. and G. Allen (Newcastle, 1891), pp. 387-394.

15. "Life of Joe Wilson," Joe Wilson, *Tyneside Songs and Drolleries* (Newcastle, n. d. [1890]), pp. xvii-xlii.

16. *Curiosities of Street Literature* (London, 1871), pp. i-ii.

17. The authorship of the original "Jone o' Grinfilt" is under some dispute. For the best known account, see John Harland and T. T. Wilkinson, eds. *Ballads and Songs of Lancashire, Ancient and Modern*, 3rd ed. (London, 1882), pp. 162-175. For a correction of this, see Charles Higson, " 'Jone o' Grinfilt' and 'Oldham Rushbearing'," Oldham *Standard*, May 1926. Ewen McColl recorded a version of "Jone o' Grinfilt, Jr." known as "The Four Loom Weaver" in the 1950's from a power loom weaver of Delph, near Oldham, See *The Shuttle and Cage* (London, 1954), p. 3.

18. For a full account of this strike and other early miners' union strikes, see Richard Fynes, *The Miners of Northumberland and Durham* (Sunderland, 1873).

19. For the details of this event I am indebted to Dr. Norman McCord, University of Newcastle, who lent me an unpublished draft of his paper "The Murder of Nicholas Fairles, Esq., J.P., at Jarrow Slake on 11th June 1832."

SUGGESTED READING

The fullest account of broadside sellers that we have is Henry Mayhew's detailed description of London sellers in the first volume of *London Labour and the London Poor*. In addition to this work and the others cited above, the reader may be interested in the following:

1. *The Common Muse*, eds. V. de Sola Pinto and A. E. Rodway (London, 1957).

2. A. L. Lloyd, *Come All Ye Bold Miners: Ballads and Songs of the Coalfields* (London, 1952).

3. A. L. Lloyd, *Folk Song in England* (London, 1967).

4. *Modern Street Ballads*, ed. John Ashton (London, 1888).

5. Leslie Shepard, *The Broadside Ballad* (London, 1962).

6. Leslie Shepard, *The History of Street Literature* (London, 1973).

7. *Victorian Street Ballads*, ed. W. Henderson (London, 1938).

BLIND WILLIE.

The Honour of a LONDON PRENTICE,

Wherein is declared his matchless Manhood, and brave Adventures done by him in *Turkey*, and by what Means he married the King's Daughter of the same Country.

The First PART.

OF a LONDON Prentice,
  my Purpose is to speak,
And tell his brave Adventures,
done for his Country's sake :
Seek all the World round,
  and you shall hardly find,
A Man in Valour to exceed,
  a Prentice gallant Mind.

He was born in C   ve,
  the chief of Me.. was he,
From thence brought up to *London*,
  a Prentice for to be :
A Merchant on the Bridge,
  did like his Service so,
That for three Years his Factor,
  to *Turkey* he should go.

And in that famous Country,
  one Year he had not been,
E'er he by Tilting did maintain,
  the Honour of the *QUEEN*,
ELIZABETH his Princess,
  he nobly did make known,
To be the Phœnix of the World,
  and none but she alone.

In *Armour* richly gilded,
  well mounted on a Steed,
One Score of Knights most hardly,
  one Day he made to bleed ;
And brought them all to Ground,
  who proudly did deny,
ELIZABETH to be the Pearl,
  Of Princely Majesty.

The King of the same Country,
  thereat began to frown,
And will'd his Son there present,
  to pull this Youngster down :
Who, at his Father's Words,
  these boasting Speeches said,
Thou art a Traytor, *English Boy*,
  and hast the Traytor play'd.

I am no Boy, nor Traytor,
  Thy Speeches I defy,
For which I'll be revenged,
  upon thee by and by :
A LONDON Prentice still,
  shall prove as good a Man,
As any of your *Turkish* Knights,
  do all the best you can.

The Second PART

AND therewithal he gave him,
  a Box upon the Ear,
Which bruke his Neck asunder,
  as plainly doth appear :
Now know, proud *Turk*! quoth he,
  I am an *English Boy*,
That can, with one small Box o'th Ear,
  the Prince of *Turks* destroy.

When as the King perceived,
  his Son so strangely slain,
His Soul was more afflicted,
  with more than mortal Pain,
And in Revenge thereof,
  he swore that he should die,
The cruel'st Death that ever Man,
  beheld with mortal Eyes.

Two Lions were prepared,
  this Prentice to devour,
Near famish'd up with Hunger,
  Ten Days within a Tower :
To make them far more fierce,
  and eager of their Prey,
To glut themselves with Humane Gore,
  upon this dreadful Day.

The appointed Time of Torment,
  at length grew near at Hand,
When all the nobles Ladie,
  and Barrons of the Land,
Attended on the King,
  to see this Prentice slain,
And buried in the hungry Maws,
  of these fierce Lions twain.

Then in his Shirt of Cambrick,
  with silk most richly wrought,
This worthy *London* Prentice,
  was from his Prison brought :
And to the Lions given,
  to stanch their Hunger great,
Which had not eat, in ten Days space,
  one smallest bit of Meat.

But GOD, who knows all secrets,
  the Matter so contriv'd,
That, by this young Man's Valour,
  they were of Life depriv'd ;
But being faint for Food,
  they scarcely could withstand,
The noble Force and Fortitude,
  and Courage of his Hand.

For when the hungry Lions,
  had cast on him their Eyes,
The Elements did thunder,
  with the Eccho of their Cries :
And running all amain,
  his Body to devour,
Into their Throats he thrust his Arms,
  with all his Might and Power.

From thence, by Manly Valour,
  their Hearts he tore asunder,
And at the King he threw them,]
  to all the Peoples Wonder :
This have I done, quoth he,
  for lovely *ENGLAND's* sake,
And for my Country Maiden *QUEEN*,
  much more will undertake.

But when the King perceived,
  his wrathful *Lions* Hearts,
Afflicted with great Terror,
  his Rigour soon reverts :
And turned all his Hate,
  into Remorse and Love,
And said, it was some Angel,
  sent down from Heaven above.

No, no I am no Angel,
  the courteous young Man said,
But born in famous *ENGLAND*,
  where GOD's Word is obey'd,
Assisted by the Heavens,
  which did me thus befriend,
Or else they had most cruelly,
  brought here my Life to end.

The King, in Heart amazed,
  lift up his Hands to Heaven,
And for his foul Offences,
  did crave to be forgiven :
Believing that no Land,
  like *ENGLAND* might be seen,
No People better govern'd,
  by Virtue of a *QUEEN*.

So taking up this young Man,
  he pardon'd him his Life,
And gave his Daughter to him,
  to be his wedded Wife :
Where then they did remain,
  and live in quite Peace,
In spending of their happy Days,
  in Joy and Love's Encrease.

Sheffield : Printed by *J. Garnet*.

PLATE No. 1

POOR FLORA
ON THE
BANKS OF BOYNE.

London :—H. SUCH, Printer and Publisher,
177, Union Street, Boro'.—S.E.

I AM a youthful damsel who loves my laddy well,
My heart was always true to him, much more
than tongue can tell,
'Twas at my father's castle he gained this heart of mine,
And he tempted me to wander on the lovely banks of
Boyne.

His hair it hung in ringlets, his cheeks were like the rose
His teeth as white as ivory, his eyes as black as sloes,
His promises they seemed sincere, his aspect bold and
fine, (Boyne.
But his heart was false to Flora on the lovely banks of

He courted me awhile and he promised me to wed,
Until he gained my favours, then away from me he fled,
His love it flew like morning dew when the sun be-
gins to shine, (Boyne.
For he quite forsook his Flora on the lovely banks of

I understood my false young man to London took his way
I packed up all my jewels upon that very day :
I bade adieu to parents who now in sorrow pine,
And forsook my father's castle on the lovely banks of
Boyne.

Then hastily I posted to fair London town,
And found my love was married to a lady of renown,
You ladies guess my feelings, and may no ill design,
Attend you like young Flora on the lovely banks of
Boyne.

No more by yonder purling streams that are so far
away, (stray ;
Where me and my bonny lad o'er lovely banks did
Now in the halls of Bedlam I pass my youthful time,
'Midst iron bars and galling chains, far from the banks
of Boyne.

Fond memory it brings to mind of joys which now
are gone, (home :
The broken-hearted Flora is deserted——far from
Young maidens all be careful——mind how you pass
your time, (of Boyne.
And think of poor young Flora, from the lovely banks

SHEFFIELD
APPRENTICE.
—o∞o—

I WAS brought up in Sheffield but not of high degree,
My parents doated on me having no child but me,
I roved about for pleasure where'er my fancy led,
'Till I was bound apprentice then all my pleasure fled.

I did not like my master he did not use me well,
I made a resolution not long with him to dwell,
Unknown to my parents I then did run away,
And steered my course to London O cursed be the day.

And when I came to London, a lady met me there,
And offered me great wages to serve her for a year,
Deluded by her promises, with her I did agree,
To go with her to Holland which proved my destiny.

I had not been in Holland passing half a year,
Before my rich young mistress did love for me declare,
She said, my gold and silver, my houses and my land,
If you consent to marry me shall be at your command.

I said my loving mistress I cannot wed you now,
For I have lately promised and made a solemn vow,
To wed with lovely Polly your pretty chambermaid,
Excuse me dearest mistress she has my heart betrayed.

Then in an angry humour from me she flew away,
Resolved for my presumption to make me dearly pay,
She was so much perplexed she could not be my bride,
She said she'd seek a project to take away my life.

As she was in the garden upon a summer's day,
And viewing the flowers that were both fine and gay,
A gold ring from her finger took as I was passing by,
She slipt into my pocket and I for the same must die.

My mistress swore I'd robb'd her and quickly I was
brought,
Before a grave old justice to answer for the fault,
Long time I pleaded innocent but every hope was vain,
She swore so false against me that I was sent to gaol.

Then at the next assizes I was condemned and cast,
And presently the judge the awful sentence passed,
From thence to execution he brought me to a tree,
So God reward my mistress for she has wronged me.

All you that come to see me here before I die,
Don't laugh at my downfall nor smile at my destiny,
Believe I'm quite innocent, to the world I bid adieu,
Farewell my pretty Polly, I die for love of you.

 333.

The Jolly
GRINDER!

THERE was a jolly Grinder once,
   Lived by the river Don,
'He work'd and sang from morn to night;
   And sometimes he'd work none;
But still the burden of his song
   For ever used to be---
" 'Tis never worth while to work too long,
   For it doesn't agree with me !"

He seldom on a Monday work'd,
   Except near Christmas Day;
It was not the labour that he'd shun,
   For it was easier far than play;
But still the burden of his song
   For ever used to be---
" 'Tis never worth while to work too long,
   For it doesn't agree with me !"

A pale teetotaller chanc'd to meet
   Our grinder one fine day,
As he sat at the door with his pipe and his
     glass,
   And thus to our friend did say:
" You destroy your health and senses too;"
   Says the grinder " you're much too free,
Attend to your work, if you've ought to do,
   And don't interfere with me.

There's a many like you go sneaking about,
   Persuading beer drinkers to turn!
'Tis easier far on our failings to spout,
   Than by labour your living to earn;
I work when I like, and I play when I can,
   And I envy no man I see;
Such chaps as you won't alter my plan,
   For I know what agrees with me !"

THE
FIRST ROSE
OF
SUMMER.

Joseph Ford, Printer, 70, Pinstone
street, Sheffield.

'TWAS the first rose of summer
   That smil'd on the morn,
And blush'd thro' the trees
   As the earliest born.
It peep'd thro' the foliage
   Encircled with dew,
Unrivall'd in beauty,
   For flowers were few.

All hail to the rose bud,
   The first of its kind;
May it never be cull'd,
   E'en a fair brow to bind.
Let it bloom in its beauty,
   For short is its stay,
And when others appear
   It will wither away.

Oh! the summer may come
   With its myriad flowers,
To hang on the shrubs
   And adorn the bright bowers,
But tho' gaudier far,
   Be the hues of the rest,
The first rose of summer
   Will still be the best.

W——'s THIRTEENS.
Indicted By Five Penknife CUTLERS.

Orbe reformato, terras astrea revifet:
Redeunt Saturnia Regna, cum novo progenies cœlo demittitur alto.

THAT monfter oppreffion behold how he ftalks
Keeps picking the bones of the poor as he walks
There's not a mechanic throughout this whole land,
But what more or lefs feels the weight of his hand
That offspring of tyranny, bafenefs and pride,
Our rights hath invaded and almoft deftroy'd,
May that man be banifh'd who villainy fcreens,
Or fides with big W—— with his thirteens.
CHORUS.
And may the odd knife his great carcafe diffect,
Lay open his vitals for men to infpect,
A heart full as black as the infernal gulph,
In that greedy blood-fucking bone fcraping wolf.

This wicked diffenter expell'd his own church,
Is render'd the fubject of public reproach,
Since reprobate marks in his forehead appear'd,

We all have concluded his confcience is fear'd,
See mammon his God, and oppreffion his aim.
Hark! how the ftreets ring with his infamous name,
The boys at the playhoufe exhibit ftrange fcenes,
Refpecting big W—— with his thirteens.
And may &c.

Like Pharaoh for bafenefs that type of the d——l,
He wants to flog journeymen with rods of fteel,
And certainly would, had he got Pharaoh's pow'r,
His heart is as hard and his temper as four;
But juftice repuls'd him and fet us all free,
Like bond flaves of old, in the Year jubilee.
May thofe be tranfported or fent for marines,
That works for big W—— at his thirteens.
And may &c.

We claim as true Yorkfhire-men feave to fpeak twice,
That no man fhould work for him at any price,
Since he has attempted our lives to enthral,
And mingle our liquor with wormwood and gall.
Come Beelzebub take him with his ill got pelf,
He's equally bad, if not worfe than thyfelf:
So fhall every Cutler that honeftly means,
"Cry take away W—— with his thirteens."
And may &c.

But fee foolifh mortals! far worfe than infane,
Three fourths are return'd into Egypt again,
Altho' Pharaoh's hands they had fairly efcap'd,
Now they muft fubmit for their bones tobe fcrap'd.
Whilft they give themfelves and their all for a prey,
Let us be unanimous and jointly fay,
Succefs to our Sovereign who peaceably reigns,
But down with both W——'s twelves & thirteens.

And may the odd knife his great carcafe diffect,
Lay open his vitals for men to infpect,
A heart full as black as the infernal gulph,
In that greedy blood fucking bone fcraping wolf.

PLATE No. 4

THE
MOWER.

It was one summer's morning on the fourteenth day of May,
I met a fair maid, she ask'd my trade, I made her this reply,
For by my occupation I ramble up and down,
With my taring scythe in order to mow the meadows down

She said, my handsome young man, if a mower that you be,
I'll find you some new employment if you will go with me,
For I have a little meadow long kept for you in store,
It was on the dew, I tell you true, it ne'er was cut before.

He said, my pretty fair maid, if it is as you say,
I'll do my best endeavours in cutting of your hay,
For in your lovely countenance I never saw a frown,
So my lovely lass, I'll cut your grass, that's ne'er been trampled down.

With courage bold undaunted she took him to the ground,
With his taring scythe in hand to mow the meadow down;
He mowed from nine till breakfast time, so far beyond his skill,
He was forced to yield and quit the field, for the grass was growing still.

She says, my handsome young man, you did promise me and say
You,d do your best endeavours in cutting of the hay,
For in my little meadow, you'll ne'er find hills nor rocks,
So I pray young man don't leave me, till you see my hay in cocks,

He said, my pretty fair maid, I can no longer stay,
But I'll go to Newry, in cutting of the hay,
But if I find the grass is cut in the country where I go,
It's then perhaps I may return, your meadow for to mow.

Now her hay being in order, and harvest being all o'er,
This young man's gone and left her sad case for to deplore,
But where he's gone I do not know, so far beyond my skill,
I was forced to yield and quit the field, for grass is growing still.

THE
Jolly Driver.

I am a jolly young fellow,
  My fortune I wish to advance,
I first took up to London,
  And I next took a tour to France,
I understand all kinds of servitude,
  And every fashion so tight,
If you hire me as your coachman,
  I am a safe driver by night.
        CHORUS.
So my darling I'll go along with yon,
  Stick to you while I have life,
I would rather ten times be your coachman,
  Than tie to a drunken old wife.

Up came a lady of fashion,
  And thus unto me did say,
If I hire you as my coachman,
  You must drive me by night and by day,
Ten guineas a month I will give you
  Besides a bottle of wine,
If you keep me in plenty of drink,
  I will drive you in a new fashion style.

She brought me into the kitchen,
  Where she gave me liquors so quick,
She told me drink that in a hurry,
  She wish'd to see my driving whip;
O when that she seen it
  She eyed it with a smile,
Saying, I know by the length of your lash,
  You can drive in a new fashion style,

She bid me get into her chaise box,
  And drive both mild and discreet,
And handle my whip with much judgment,
  And drive her quite through the street,
Three curls I gave to my cracker,
  And then I was up to her rigg,
And the very first turn the wheel got,
  I broke the main-spring of her gig.

She brought me into the cellar,
  And gave me a bottle of wine,
She told me drink that in a hurry,
  As I had to drive her three miles;
She being a nice little young thing,
  And just in the height of her bloom,
And I being a dashing young fellow,
  I drove her nine times round the room.

My mistress being tired and weary,
  In order to take a rest,
She call'd for her waiting-maid, Sally,
  The maid that she loved the best,
Saying, Sally, we've got a good coachman,
  That understands driving in style,
And while my gig wheel is repairing,
  I'll let him drive you for a mile.

So now to conclude and finish,
  Driving I mean to give o'er,
Carriages, cars, gigs, and coaches,
  I ne'er will drive any more;
When the Ladies of honour all heard it,
  The truth they did declare,
They ne'er could meet with a coachman,
  That understood driving so fair.

PLATE No. 5

BOLD POACHER,

OR,

MY DELIGHT ON A SHINY NIGHT

When I was bound 'prentice in fair Lincolnshire,
I served my master for nearly seven years,
'Till I got up to poaching, as quickly you shall hear,
It was my delight in a shiny night, in the season of the
    year.

As I and my comrades were setting of a snare,
The gamekeeper was watching us, for him we did not care,
For I could wrestle or fight my boys or jump over any-
    where,   [year.
It was my delight in a shiny night, in the season of the

As I and my comrades were setting four or five,
And going to take them up again, we found a hare alive,
I have her in the bag, my boys, and through the woods
    we steer,   [year.
It was my delight in a shiny night, in the season of the

I hung her over my shoulder and rambled to the town,
I called at a neighbour's house and sold her for a crown
I sold her for a crown my boys, but I never told you
    where,   [year
It was my delight in a shiny night, in the season of the

Here's to every poacher that lives in Lincolnshire,
And here's to every gamekeeper that wants to buy a
    hare,
But now to every keeper that wants to keep his deer,
It was my delight in a shiny night, in the season of the
    year.

24

Cadman, Printer, 152, Gt. Ancoats, Manchester.

THE SAILOR'S
RETURN

As a fair maid walked in a garden,
  A brisk young sailor chanced to spy,
He stept up to her thinking to have her,
  And said fair maid can you fancy I.

You appear to be a man of honour,
  A man of honour you appear to be,
How can you impose on a poor woman,
  Who is not fit your servant to be.

If you are not fit to be my servant,
  I have a sincere regard for you,
I would marry and make you a lady,
  For I have servants to wait on you.

I have a true sweetheart of my own,
  It is seven years since he was gone,
And seven years more I will wait for him,
  For if he's living he will return.

'Tis seven years since your lover left you,
  I'm sure he's either dead or drown'd,
If he's living I love him dearly,
  If he's dead with glory he's crown'd.

When he perceived her love was loyal,
  It is a pity true love should be cross'd,
Says he I am thy poor and single sailor,
  Who has often on the ocean been toss'd.

If you are my poor and single sailor,
  Shew me the token you gave to me,
For seven years it makes an alteration,
  Since my true lover has parted from me

He pull'd his hand out of his bosom,
  His fingers being long and small,
Saying here's the ring we broke between us
  When she saw it down she did fall.

Then he lifted her up clasped in his arms,
  And gave her kisses one two and three
Saying I am thy poor and single sailor,
  Who is just returned to marry thee.

New
Bury Loom

As I walked between Bolton and Bury,
  It was on a moon shiny night,
I met with a buxom young weaver,
  Whose company gave me delight:
She says, my young fellow come tell me
  If your level and rule are in tune,
Come give me an answer correct,
  Can you get up and square my new loom.

I said, dear lassie believe me,
  I am a good joiner by trade,
And many a good loom and shuttle
  Before in my time I have made.
Your short lams and jacks and long lams,
  I quickly can put them in tune,
My rule is now in good order,
  To get up and square a new loom.

She took me and shewed me her new loom,
  The down on her warp did appear,
The lamb jacks and healds put in motion,
  I leveled her loom to a hair,
My shuttle run well in her lathe,
  My treadle it did up and down,
My level stood next to her breast-beam,
  The time I was squaring her loom.

The cords of my lamb jacks and treadles,
  At length they began to give way,
The bobbin I had in my shuttle,
  The weft on it no longer would stay :
Her lathe it went bang to and fro,
  My main treadle still kept in tune,
My pickers went nickety nack,
  All the time I was squaring her loom.

My shuttle it still kept in motion,
  Her lams she worked well up and down,
The weights in her rocs they did tremble,
  She said she would have a new gown,
My strength now began for to fail me,
  I said its now right to a hair,
She turned up her eyes and said Tommy,
  My loom you have got very square.

But when the fore-loom-post she let go,
  It flew out of order amain,
She cried, bring your rule and your level,
  And help me to square it again.
I said my dear lassie I'm sorry,
  At Bolton I must be by noon,
But when I come back this way,
  I will square up your jerry hand loom.

PLATE NO. 7

THE
ORIGINAL
JONE
O' GRINFIELD !

Says Jone to his wife on a hot summers day,
Aw'm determined in Greenfield no longer to stay,
So aw'll go to Owdham as fast as aw con,
So fare thee weel Greenfield & fare thee weel Nan
For a solder I'st be un brave Owdham Is't see,
An awll have a battle with French.

Says my Aunt Margart I'd ne'er be so hot,
I'd ne'er go to Owdham in England I'd stop ;
It matters nowt Margart a very weel know,
As't ne'er clem to deoth by some one shall know,
First Frenchman aw find aw'll tell him mi mind
And if he'll not fight let him run.

Dear Jone said ar Nan, and hoo bitterly cried,
Wilta' be one oth foot or tha meous for to ride,
Egad aw'll either ride a ass or a mule,
I'll naer stop i'Grinfield as black as a dule,
For we're clamming & starving & never a fartling
It's enough to drive only mon mad.

So aw went down th' broo for wo lived at th' top,
Aw swore awd reach Owdham afore ere aw'd stop,
Lord hew they start'd when a geet to the Mumps,
Wi'ny hat i' mi hont and mi' clogs full o'stumps,
But very soon towd um that a were goin' to
            Owdham,
An aw'd have a battle with French.

Whan aw' geet into Owdham up street sw went,
A ax't recuit if he'd made up his keawnt,
He said, no, honest lad theaw talks like a king,
And if you'll go wi' mi' thee aw will bring
And if th'w art willing theaw may have a shil'ing
I gad aw thawt that wur rare new.

He took me to th' pleck where thep measured
            their hesght,
And if they be length they sen nowtabout weight
A retched me' and stretched mi' an never flinch,
Egad he says lad theawrt me height to an inch,
Thinks aw tnat'll do aw'st have a guinea coat,
Egad Owdham brave Owdham for me.

Fare thee weel Grinfield to order am made,
Awve getten new shoon an a rare Cockade,
Aw'll fight for owd England as hard as a con,
Either French, Dutch, or Spanish to meits all,
Aw'll mak um to stare like a new started hare,
And aw'll tell um fro Owdham aw'm come.

MANCHESTER:
T. Pearson, Printer, 4 & 6, Chadderton Street

GOD BLESS
THE EARL OF
SHAFTESBURY

OW once I was a helpless child,
    And no protector nigh ;
To teach me honesty to live,
    And yet I ne'er shall die;
But the noble Earl of Shaftesbury
    At last la d down to rule,
To teach the London Aarbs,
    And fremed a Ragged School.

CHORUS:

Oh! bless the Earl of Shaftesbury.
    And the must be great fools!
Who would not praise the man that raised,
    Our British Ragged School.

How oft tha Catherine when I've turned,
    To a company on a bus ;
And strove to get a copper,
    To earn myself a crust,
But now the case is altered,
    We think Miss Burdett Cutts.
For if peace you give us to live,
    In return we clean your boots.

Next draft there is I hound for sea,
    To seve sur gracious Queen !
But not her shoes to brush,
    But her British Bull Dogs cleanl
And defy merit I should raise,
    Which should always be the plan,
I'll shout harrah! for Shaftsbury,
    Who made me a honest me.

We've no Collingwood or Nelson now,
    Wherein does the the faul,
It is the beard of Admeralty,
    ' Or oxr commissioners bought,
Tis not the Lord high Admiral,
    But his unproved crews,
How often would they clean his hoots,
    To walk into his shoes.

I'm thankful for my station,
    And my letters don't abuse,
Perhaps in time in life's decline,
    Some one may my shoes,
Equality is all my eyes,
    It makef men worse than brutes,
For if Equal all no one at all,
    Would ever clean your boots.

JONE O'GRINFIELD.

I'm a poor cotton weaver as many one knows,
I've nowt to eat i'th house an I've worn out my cloas,
You'd hardly give sixpence for all I have on,
My clugs they are brossen and stockings I've none,
You'd think it wur hard to be sent into th' world,
    To clem and do th' best ot you con.

Our church parson kept telling us long,
We should have better times if we'd hold our tongues,
I've houden my tongue till I can hardly draw breath,
I think i' my heart he means to clem me to death;
I know he lives weel by backbiting the de'il,,
    But he he never pickced o'er in his life.

I tarried six week an thought every day wur t' last,
I tarried and shifted till now I'm quite fast;
I lived on nettles while nettles were good,
An Waterloo porridge were best of my food;
I'm telling you true I can find folks enew,
    That are living no better than me.

Old Bill o' Dan's sent bailiffs one day,
For a shop score I owed him that I could not pay,
But he wur too late for old Bill o' Bent,
Had sent tit and cart and taen goods for rent,
We had nou bur a stoo, that wur a seat for two,
    And on it cowered Margit and me.

The bailiffs looked round assly as a mouse,
When they saw aw things were taen out ot house,
Says one to the other all's gone thou may see,
Aw sed lads never fret you're welcome to me;
They made no more ado, but nipp'd up th' owd stoo,
    And we both went wack upoth flags.

I geet howd of Margit for hoo wur strucken sick,
Hoo sed hoo ne'er had such a bang sin hoo wur wick
The bailiffs scoured off with owd stoo on their backs,
They would not have cared had they brook our necks,
They're mad at owd Bent cos he's taen goods for rent,
    And wur ready to flee us alive.

I sed to our Margit as we lay upoth floor,
We shall never be lower in this world I'm sure,
But if we alter I'm sure we mun mend ,
For I think in my heart we are both at far end,
For meat we have none nor looms to weave on,
    Egad they're as weel lost as found.

Then I geet up my piece and I took it em back
I scarcely dare speak mester looked so black,
He said you wur o'erpaid last time you coom,
I said if I wur 'twas for weaving bout loom;
In a mind as I'm in I'll ne'er pick o'er again,
    For I've woven mysel toth' fur end.

Then aw coom out and left him to chew that,
When aw thought again aw wur vext till aw sweat,
To think that we mun work to keep them and awth set,
All the day o' my life and still be in their debt;
So I'll give o'er trade an work with a spade,
    Or go and break stones upoth road,

Our Margit declared if hoo'd cloas to put on,
Hoo'd go up to Lundun an see the big mon
An if things didn't alter when hoo had been,
Hoo swears hoo'd feight blood up toth e'en,
Hoo's nought again th' Queen but likes a fair thing,
    An hoo says hoo can tell when hoo's hurt.

SALLY SLY.

Printed and Sold Wholesale and Retail, by
    gton   den-street, Oldham
Road, Manchester.

At six in the morning awaking,
    Coals taking,
    Love making,
        With barrow, I cry;
I knock and sing at the areas,
    My care is
    The fairies,
        With coals to supply.

I'm in love! I'm in love! Oh my eye!
I'm going for to meet her to-morrow—
Sally Sly! Sally Sly! Sally Sly!
I'm going for to meet her to-morrow—
Sally Sly! Sally Sly! Sally Sly!

We meet where the walls they've been
    While walking   (chalking,
    And talking;
        We're both tall and straight,
With apples and cherries I treat her
    Sweet creature,
    I meet her
    To-morrow, at eight.
I'm in love, &c.

One day, Jemmy Raspell, the baker,
    To take her
    And make her
    His tool, he did try;
He told her to kick Jemmy Snivel
    To the devil—
    How civil;
    Then she blacken'd his eye.
I'm in love, &c.

32.

Then Sir, our Tythes. **Our Pensions?** **Huzza! Reform.**

A laughable & interesting Dialogue, between Joan o'Greenfield,
NOSEY AND EARL GREY.

Nosey.—WELL, my good man, what is your will, have you some petitions to leave?

Joan.—Now mon, its not fustian aw weav, its cotton; I thout yod knone as I cum up to luck for a job, as yort hed mon.

Nosey.—You are wrong, I am not head man; I resigned my situation to Earl Grey, it is him, I dare say, you are wanting.

Joan.—Nay, I think aum reight, yort' hed mon at Borohmungering set, yor caud Nosey, ats got 1,000,000 pewnds frat country.

Nosey.—Tell me your business man; what I have got I intend to keep; what is the job you are wanting, or looking for?

Joan.—Why, the job I'm looking for, is to get to hang yo Boroughmongers, now 't Bill's passed, for if sumbody dos'nt hang yo, yole be cutting yore throits.

Nosey.—I tell you, fellow, I have given up, nor is it my intention again to interfere with Reform.

Joan.—If thau had given up afore, it would have been better for yo, but if they dunna hang yo felleys, I hope tey'll send yo where tha sent aud Boney, for yor bigger tyrants tan him, dust tew think yo isnt, Nosey?

Nosey.—Confusion to the fellow, am I to be tormented in this manner? I have filled the first offices of State, and must I thus be abused for my services.

Joan.—Hey, an thau fill'd thy pockets at same time thr' knose! but if t' aud felley dust'nt torment tha worse tan me, aum mista'n then—but aul go an see Earl Grey, and talk to him abewt yo.—Exit Joan.

E. Grey.—Well John, I am happy to see you, what is your business pray?

Joan.—Well, auv cum up to Lunnun abewt Reform Bill, an I hear at aud Nosey shuv'd yo ewt, an shuv'd his nose in; auv bin tokin to him abewt it.

Grey.—Well John, I am happy to tell you, that the Reform Bill is in a fair way; I have only accepted my office, upon conditions of carrying it.

Joan.—Well, thew'rt a gradely chap after o', an if ivver yo cum into Lungcasher, yost hev best to yeat ith' hewse; an if yo dunnat loik jonnack, awst get best breade and bear for yo ith' country;—but con yo tell me when ther going to hong t' Burrowmongers?

Grey.—Their Salaries will be instantly reduced, John they will not hang them, but they will be so put under, that they will not have the least power to harm us.

Joan.—Yo man put 'em undert' grewnd ten, but I understond tev'r goin to stop their porrige, to fetch Burrowmungers' guts dewn abit; what think yo abewt it, dunnot yo think its gradely?

Grey.—It is right, John, for the voice of the People is the voice of God, nor can they longer refuse the " People's Rights," when they are unanimous and determined!

Joan.—Well, aum glad to think yo've dun um so, an when their big guts has cumd dewn, now th' Reform Bill passed, I hope yo'll tell aud Nosey an th' Bis——ps ta cum inta Lungcasher, an we'll make em weivers ;—but aul sing yo a song, that seys moor abewt it.

COME Britons all rejoice and sing,
For Nosey thought he would be king,
But the British voice aloud did ring,
And Nosey swore 'twas thunder!
We are undone, Old Nosey cries,
The people they do us despise,
Let us resign, or they will rise,
And sure I am they'll us chastise.
So Bobby, Nosey, and his crew,
They scarcely knew what way to do,
And some of them they say did spew,
And I'm sure it was no wonder.
CHORUS.
Harum, scarum, Nosey run,
Rantum, tarum, scratchum, mam,
Old Nosey cries, we are undone,
I've made a cursed blunder.
The B——ps too, cried out aloud,
Let all of us prepare our shroud,

I'm sure we'll die, this cursed crowd
Are come our tythes to plunder.
No more we'll revel on our spoil,
Nor cheat the poor man of his toil,
Nor widows' pigs no more shall boil,
For all our dev'lish schemes they'll foil,
Let us pack up and run away,
I'm sure no longer we can stay,
For they do swear they'll have fair play,
And tear our tythes asunder.
So now they see we're fully bent,
To have REFORM in Parliament;
Likewise free trade is our intent,
Throughout the British Nation.
Through all the Nation we will join,
That every man may have his own,
For Nosey and his crew we scorn;
In spite of them we've gain'd Reform.
Britannia now all Tyrants braves,

Her sons no longer shall be slaves,
But with free trade she rules the waves,
In spite of Tory Placemen?
Hully, bully, romp and tear,
Women should not breeches wear,
A broomstick is not made of hair,
Or Dublin's not in Ireland.
So to conclude and finish off,
Of Taxes there has been enough,
But now REFORM we have got proof
Becomes the Law of England.
Our children shall speak of these days,
And likewise sound their fathers' praise,
And tell their young ones of the ways,
We did get clear of tythes and leys :—
So Britons let us all rejoice,
For Earl Grey is the people's choice,
And Nosey trembled at his voice,
The humbug tool of England.

SHEFFIELD : *W. Ford, Printer, York-Street,*

FAIR PHŒBE,
AND HER
Dark-Eyed
SAILOR.

Printed, and Sold Wholesale and Retail, by G. Jacques, Oldham Road Library, Manchester.

IT'S of a comely young lady fair
Was walking out to take the air,
She met with a sailor upon her way,
So I paid attention to hear what they did say.

Said William, lady why, roam alone,
The night is coming, and the day near gone,
She said, while tears from her eyes did fall,
It's a dark-eyed sailor that's proving my downfall

It's two long years since he left the land,
I took a gold ring from off my hand,
We broke the token—here's part with me
And the other rolling at the bottom of the sea.

Said William drive him from your min
Some other sailor as good you'll find,
Love turns aside, and soon cold does grow,
Like a winter's morning when lands are clothed
with snow.

These words did Phœbe's fond heart inflame,
She said on me you shall play no game,
She drew a dagger and then did cry,
For my dark-eyed sailor, a maid I'll live and die

His coal-black eye, and his curly hair,
And pleasing tongue did my heart ensnare,
Genteel he was but no rake like you,
To advise a maiden to slight the jacket blue.

But still said Phœbe I'll ne'er disdain
A tarry sailor, but treat the same,
Drink his health—here's a piece of coin,
But my dark-eyed sailor still claims this heart
of mine.

Then half the ring did young William show,
She seemed distracted 'midst joy and woe,
Oh, welcome William, I've lands and gold,
For my dark-eyed sailor, so manly true & bold.

Now in a village down by the sea-side,
They're joined in wedlock, and well agree,
So maids be true when your love's away,
For a cloudy morning oft brings a pleasant day

Fortunate
FACTORY GIRL.

Printed, and Sold Wholesale and Retail, by G. Jacq
Oldham Road Library, Manchester.

THE sun had just risen one fine summer's morning,
When the birds from the bushes so sweetly did sing
When the lads and the lasses so merrily moving,
Unto those large buildings their labour begins;
I espied a fair damsel, far brighter than Venus,
Her cheeks red as roses none could her excel,
With a skin like a lily that grows in the garden,
Had this lovely young goddess, a factory girl

I stepped up to her, this beautiful creature,
She cast upon me a proud look of disdain:
Stand back, sir, she cried, and do not insult me,
Though poor and in poverty, that is no sin,
I said, my sweet damsel, no harm is intended,
But grant me one favour, pray where do you dwell,
At home, sir, she answer'd, and was going to leave me
I am only a hard working factory girl.

I stood all amazed. and at her I gazed,
Such modesty and prudence, I never did see,
You are my sweet charmer, my soul's great armer,
If you will consent, you a lady shall be,
But she said, sir, temptations are used in all stations
Go marry a lady and you will do well:
So let me alone, sir, the bell is a ringing,
I am only a hard working factory girl.

I stood in a flutter, knew not what was the matter,
Little Cupid the whole of my heart it trepann'd,
Lovely girl I replied, if you'll not be my bride,
My life I will waste in some foreign land,
For what pleasure's in treasure when love is a wanting,
Your beauty upon me it has cast a spell;
I'll marry you speedy, and make you a lady,
If you will become mine, dear factory girl.

She gave her consent, when a license was purchased
The bells they did merrily echo and ring;
To church then they went, and as they return'd
They bride's men and maidens so sweetly did sing
Now this loving young couple live happy together,
She blesses the day that she met with her swain,
So this factory girl she is made a great lady,
And married to a squire of honour and fame.

[No. 61.]

OWDHAM STREETS
AT DINNER TIME.

In Owdham streets at dinner time
　　The workfolk how they flock,
Just as you hear the church clock chime
　　Each day at half-past twelve o'clock.
In such a hurry crowds you meet
At the turn of every street;
You'd think all t' world, as I'm a sinner,
Wur come to Owdham o' getting their dinner.

If you go to th' bottom o' th' moor,
　　That's thongest place i' th' town,
When all those factories work give o'er,
　　The crowds will nearly nock you down:
The spinner then can leave his wheel
To get a comfortable meal;
And tell his piecer t' not off wander,
But look sharp back and get clean'd under.

There's Jones', Bell's, and castle mill,
　　Gleadhill's and Hillon's send out their ranks;
Till half-past one they're never still—
　　It's like a fair at Lousey Banks.
The lasses then, who think they're fair,
Blackball their heels and curl their hair,
Sayin', " Put up my hair nicely Nelly,
For to day at noon I'st meet my felly."

There's Scholes' and the Union too,
　　With Broadbent's make a decent stock;
From Seville's and Wright's there is a few
　　Turn out at half-past twelve o'clock:
There's Barlow's and Cowper's German mill,
Ratcliffe's and Hague's a church would fill;
Fro' Collins' and Lancashire's out they rally,
And then make up fro' John's-o'-Sally's.

If you stop at th' Lackey Moor,
　　rOf foundry men you'll see a flock;
Fom Barns's and Hibbert's and Platt's some
　　　　scores
　　Turn out at half-past twelve o'clock:
The moulder then he leaves his sand—
Th' mechanic leads up rest o' th' band;
A man would think they're ruuning races,
For they're every one gone black i' their faces.

On Monday at noon, when th' mill's all stop,
　　The lasses come up to th' town in flocks,
To see what's fresh in each ffne shop,
　　Just takes till half-past one o'clock:
Th're buying some smart thing at last,
When who but th' chap by chance comes past,
gested Then o'th' bargain how they clack again,
　　　th're off like good un's when th' bells ring
　　　　ack again.

PLATE No. 12

Sam Shuttle
AND BETTY
Reedhook.

I'm going for to give you
A very strange narration ;
But what I tell is really true,
Of my own observation.
A lass there was and as nice a one
As any on you'd need look,
She was a steam loom weaver,
And they called her Betty Reedhook.
  Tow, row, row, &c.

There was a chap in love with her,
He said quite to distraction,
And wanted ill to marry her
In spite of all objection ;
This was an overlooker,
That came oft her loom to fettle,
He work'd at th' top oth' Lacky Moor,
And they call'd him Sommy Shuttle.
  Tow, row, row, &c;

Now Betty could n't bear this chap,
Tho' some fine things he took her,
A spark ith' warehouse won her, slap,
He wur a sly Cut Looker ;
And when she took her cuts to him,
They'd so much fun and prate, sir,
He always past o'er all her faults,
And never used to bate her.
  Tow, row, row, &c.

When Sam yeard o' these going on,
In a grate passion he flies up,
Swearin' if he met that mon
He'd smartly knock his eyes up.
A challenge then he sent to him,
For on killin' him he reckon'd,
And he'd take wi' him Billy Crape,
And he should act as second.
  Tow, row, row, &c.

Th' Cut Looker said he'd fight the man,
In any part oth' town, sir ;
If it must be on th' Oldham plan,
A regular up and down, sir.
So at Lacky Moor they did meet,
That same afternoon, sir,
And Sam geet half a pound o' stumps
Put into his new shoon, sir.
  Tow, row, row, &c.

Sam first took a punce at him,
But th' Cut Looker he legg'd him,
Gan him some cross buttockers,
And down to th' floor he pegg'd him ;
He geet his fingers in his throat,
And twisted o'er so nimbly,
That Sam at last wur forced t' give in
When he fund he'd stopp'd his chimbly.
  Tow, row, row, &c.

VERSES ON THE EXECUTION
OF
CATHERINE FOSTER'
FOR POISONING HER HUSBAND

Harkness, Printer, 121, Church Street, Preston.

The solemn knell does most awful sound
Oh God in pity on me look down,
Forgive my sins and compassion take,
And grant me fortitude to meet my fate.

Oh what numbers approach to see
A wretched female upon the tree,
My time is come and I must be soon,
A prey to worms in the silent tomb.

When I was scarce eighteen years of age,
To wed John Foster I did engage,
He unto me was both good and kind,
But murder entered my wicked mind.

We married had been but three weeks,
When to take his life I a plan did seek,
I poured some poison one fatal day,
And with the same took his life away.

When from his labour he did return,
To see him suffer my heart did burn,
He took the poison right speedily,
But little thinking he was to die.

Though I married him I did not him like,
That was the reason I took his life,
That was the reason I did him kill,
Maidens never marry against your will.

My bosom heaves and borne down with woe,
The grave lies open and I must go,
To sleep with death till the Judgement day,
When God will pardon me I firmly pray.

It was cursed Satan led me astray,
It was Satan tempted me one day,
It was Satan prompted my guilty mind,
To slay a husband both good and kind.

Young men and maidens ere 'tis too late,
Oh take a warning by my fate,
Trust in your Saviour who reigns above,
And never wed whom you cannot love.

It was well for me had I never been born,
To die a death of public scorn,
In youth and bloom on the fatal tree,
Oh God in mercy look down on me.

Petitions have in my favour been
Sent from Bury town to my gracious Queen,
But alas no mercy is there for me,
And I must die on the fatal tree.

Three weeks I have lain in a gloomy cell
Where my dreadful sufferings no one can tell,
To gain me pardon my friends have tried,
But oh alas, it has been denied.

When Betty yeard that Sam had lost,
On him no notice took, sir,
But went walkin' out on Sunday last,
With that sly old Cut Looker.
Sam swore he could not stand it,
And on 'em no more he'd look,
He'd blow his brains out wi' his Shuttle
Or stab him wi' his Reedhook.
  Tow, row, row, &c.

PLATE No. 13

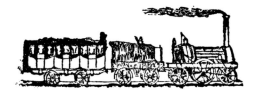

NAVVY ON THE LINE

I am a navvy bold, that has tramp'd the country round, sir,
For to get a job of work where any can be found, sir,
I left my native home, my friends and my relations,
To ramble up and down the town and work in various stations

CHORUS.

I am a navvy don't you see, I love my beer in all my prime,
Because I am a navvy that is working on the line.

I left my native home on the first of September,
That memorable day I still do remember,
I bundled up my kit put on my smock and Sunday cap, sir,
And wherever I do ramble, folks call me happy Jack sir.

I have got a job of work all in the town of Bury,
And working on the line is a thing that makes me merry,
I can use my pick and spade, and my wheelbarrow,
And I can court the lasses too, but never intend to marry.

I worked a fortnight, and then it came to pay day,
And when I geet my wages I thought I'd have a play day,
And then to a little spree in Clark street went quite handy,
And I sat me down in Jenkinson's beside a Fanny Brandy.

I called for a pint of beer, and bid the old wench drink, sir,
But while she were drinking, she too at me did wink, sir,
Then we had some talk and in the backside we had a rally,
Then we jump'd over brush and steel and agreed to live tally.

They called for liquors merrily the jugs went quickly round sir,
Oh, that being my wedding day I spent many a crown sir,
But when my brass was all done old Fanny went a cadging,
And for to finish up the spree I went and sloped my lodging.

O, now my chaps, I am going to leave the town of Bury,
And I am sorry for to leave you for I always found you merry,
But now I call for liquors merry and drink away my dandy
And cry out here's health to happy Jack and Fanny Brandy.

I am a navvy, don't you see loves my beer all in my prime,
For it's I'm a navvy, bold, that's working on the line.

Cadman, Printer, 152, Gt. Ancoats, Manchester.

198

DRUNKEN HUSBAND.

You married women draw near awhile,
I'll tell you a tale that will make you smile,
Concerning a man and a wife you see,
Who after they married could never agree.

CHORUS.

So women I hope you'll follow this plan,
If you should be plagued with a drunken man,

This couple got married for better or worse,
But the wife had reason the man for to curse,
For never could he give her a good word,
But at night comes home as drunk as a lord.

One morning a scheme came into her head,
Whilst he was drinking she pawn'd the bed,
When he came home he began to rant & roar,
But that night he was forced to lie on the floor.

Next morning early, she went in a flirt,
And pawn'd his waistcoat, breeches, and shirt,
And before she returned home again,
She spent three parts of the money in gin.

He put on his rags and went afloat,
She went and sold his hat and coat,
She went where he was, and he did her abuse,
Then he spouted his stockings and shoes.

He came home at night in a terrible rage,
But she was ready the foe to engage,
She plucked up her spirits and he did begin,
She knocked him down with the rolling pin.

I'll serve you out to her he said,
She up with the poker and cracked his head,
She cries you villain I'll serve you out,
She wollop'd him well with the dirty clout.

He hallooed aloud, she tore his clothes,
She black'd his eye and broke his nose,
You villain she cries none of your airs,
Then slap she tumbled him over the stairs.

Dear wife, dear wife, he then did say,
On your husband have compassion I pray,
And if my dear you'll me now forgive,
I'll never get drunk as long as I live.

I'll forgive you she cried and opened the door,
If you'll promise to never get drunk any more,
He took an oath and ended the strife,
And now they live happy like man and wife.

He never gets drunk, his wife he loves,
And they live together like turtle doves,
So women you'll find this an excellent plan,
If you wish to reform a drunken man.

PLATE No. 14

GIBBETING
OF THE
OF
William Jobling,
AT JARROW SLAKE,

On Monday, August 6th, 1832, pursuant to his Sentence, for the Murder of Nicholas Fairles, Esq., resident Magistrate of South Shields, with a correct Representation of the Gibbet.

After the body of Jobling had hung on the drop at Durham for an hour, it was taken down, the clothes were stripped off, but no incision made, it was covered over with pitch, and the cloths in which he was hung-ed were then replaced.

On Monday morning, at 7 o'clock, the body was brought in a small four-wheeled waggon, drawn by two horses, from Durham, escorted by a troop of the 8th hussars, and two companies of the 18th regiment of Infantry, Mr Griffiths, the under-sheriff, Mr Flushard, the gaoler, officers of the gaol, bailiffs &c. &c.

They proceeded by way of Chester-le-street, Pictree, Sludge Row, Portobello, over the Black Fell, to White Mare Pool, and thence, by the South Shields turnpike road, to Jarrow Slake, where they arrived at half-past one o'clock. The spectators were not numerous perhaps 1000 in number, and not many pitmen amongst them; arising, probably, from a meeting ... held by them that day on Bowden Fell.

... of the Cavalcade at Jarrow Slake it ... Abbs, and Wm. Loraine Esqrs.

... drawn up, and formed two ... on the right and the

... waggon. It was ... breadth. The ... ar of iron ... collar

thighs, the bowels, the breast, and the shoulders; the hands were hung by the side and covered with pitch; the face was pitched and covered with a piece of white cloth. being laid on a hand barrow, the body was fixed nearly opposite the spot where the murder was committed, and about 60 yards from high water mark.

The gibbet is formed of a square piece of oak, 21 feet long, and about three feet in diameter, with strong bars of iron up each side. It is fixed in a stone 1¾ ton weight, which is sunk in the Slake. At high water there will be 16 or 17 feet of the gibbet visible.

The body was then hoisted up and secured, and left as a warning for the futer, and a memento of the past.

There will be Military guard on the spot for a fortnight.

The procession passed on its route without the least interruption; and on the spot, every thing was quiet and orderly. One solitary voice only, as they carried the body from the waggon to the gibbet, shouted out "take the police with him, over the water."

The following Handbill was distributed in Shields and the neighbourhood:—

NOTICE TO THE PUBLIC.—In the Act of Parliament ordering the dead Bodies of Murderers to be hung in Chains, there is a Clause inflicting the Punishment of Transportation for seven Years, upon all who may be guilty of Stealing the Body from the Gibbet.

Joseph Barker & the Socialists.

Lines showing how the Socialists would not meet Joseph Barker in a discussion at Bradford.

Once more Reuben Holder doth take up his pen,
To write a few lines on those poor silly men
The socialists, those cowards and shufflers, I say,
Before Joseph Barker they're forced to give way.

Joseph Barker has tried them for twelve months and
    more
To hold a discussion with them o'er and o'er;
He tried many times and offered so fair,
But Socialists, like cowards, they durst not come there.

Like a true hearted champion, J. Barker, he came
To open the cause; and the Socialist's aim
To get all the money where ever they could,
Likewise to deceive you by sucking your blood.

'Tis true they have told you oft times they did plan
To hold a discussion, they'd ready a man;
But, when they were proved, no man could be found
To face Joseph Barker upon a fair ground.

He sendeth a letter, unto them he says,
Bring forth your man within eighteen days,
But if any more you shuffle again,
With such as you are I wont bother my brain.

But did they come forward? No, no, they did not,
They then were to seek—no man had they got;
So Barker will have no more of their game,
To have a discussion his labour's in vain.

Away with such doctrines belonging to Owen,
They are not worth notice to you I am showing;
Give over your balls, and such wicked play,
And then your system will soon die away.

On Wednesday night, Joseph Barker did prove
True godliness unto believers was love;
To love one another is worshiping God,
Believing in Jesus and his precious blood.

But old Owen's system is nothing but evil,
'T will lead you, if follow'd, headlong to the devil;
They talk about God with a sneering and joke,
Make game of the bible—that blessed good book.

Their words and their ways would make you to shame,
They wish that the bible were all in a flame;
They say that the bible doth make a man mad,
It teaches him nothing but evil and bad.

In old Owen's books you there may behold
How they are contriving to get all your gold;
A New Moral World they are trying to make,
To surpass the old world if they dont mistake.

This New Moral World, I'd have you to read,
They tell you a man is to have all he need,
Both eating and drinking, apparel to wear,
Like gentry they say you will always appear.

But mark, before you with them can go live,
You fifty bright pounds unto them must give,
The same for your wife and each loving child,
So keep your money and be reconciled.

And should you go there, beware what I say,
Your poor little children are taken away;
Then William and Mary no longer are thine,
And thy wife another can choose any time.

And in that New World thou loses thy powers,
There nothing is thine, thou says it is ours;
There will be no money, but such meat and cheer,
And if thou do grumble they'll send thee elsewhere.

In Wakefield treadmill poor criminals have got
Apparel and eating served out in a lot;
And if they do speak, to the dungeon they're sent,
And make them obey to their government.

And so will the Owenites when they get you,
Whatever they say you must instantly do;
And should you refuse you soon will be made,
Or leave the community and what you have paid.

So keep from these swindlers and deceiving knaves,
Before they transport you and make you like slaves;
So take my advice, stop here while you may,
And do not your money to Owenites pay.

They're nothing but infidels under a cloak,
They try our good men to grieve and provoke;
They'll lead your children, self, and your wife
To hell and destruction when done in this life.

Mark you, on a death bed when infidels lie,
They're weeping and wailing, for mercy they cry;
Believe in the Lord whatever beside,
Then you will die shouting the Lord will provide.

W. & H. Byles, Printers, Bradford.

PLATE NO. 16

THE KING
OF THE
FACTORY CHILDREN

Friends, stop and listen unto me,
While I give a brief history
Of one who's gain'd his liberty,
    The King of the Factory Children.
Of Richard Oastler now I sing,
Let all good men their laurels bring,
And deck them round their old tri'd King,
    The King of the Factory Children.
Let each one with his neighbour vie,
And shout his praises to the sky,
For labours past to gratify,
    The King of the Factory Children.
        CHORUS.
Rejoice, Rejoice, the time has come,
The Captive's left his dungeon gloom
Amongst his subjects for to roam,
    The King of the Factory Children.

His sterling worth I can't unfold,
He's made oppression loose its hold,
His labours can't be bought for gold,
    The King of the Factory Children.
A terror to tyrants and to knaves,
Protector of the Factory slaves,
To pluck them hence from premature graves,
    The King of the Factory Children.
His time and talents he did spend,
His factory subjects to defend,
To save them from a cruel end,
    The King of the Factory Children.

To limit the hours of Factory toil,
He stood undaunted 'midst the broil,
Of those who strove the work to foil,
    Of the King of the Factory Children.
But infants' labour was curtail'd,
And petty tyrants writh'd and wail'd,
With oaths and curses they assail'd
    The King of the Factory Children.
But gratitude the chain has broke,
Which bound him to the tyrant's yoke,
The prison-house no more's the walk
    Of the King of the Factory Children.

The "Bastile Laws" he did oppose,
For he foresaw the poor man's woes,
He therefore stood to plead their cause,
    The King of the Factory Children;
For man and wife to parted be,
Against Almighty God's decree,
For no "crime," but poverty,
    He could not tamely sit to see:
He told the rich with all his might,
To rob the poor they had no right,
Which thunder'd down the tyrants' spite,
    At the King of the Factory Children.

The "Lord of Fixby" him confin'd,
Four years to burk his noble mind,
But all could not the influence bind
    Of the King of the Factory Children:
His "Fleeters" flew from south to north,
To east and west they issued forth,

And each proclaim'd the sterling worth
    Of the King of the Factory Children.
Now from his prison-house he's come,
His arduous labours to resume
And tyrants they will hear their doom,
    From the King of the Factory Children.

Now loyal subjects all agree,
And cheer your King with three times three,
That's now restor'd to liberty,
    The King of the Factory Children.
And shew the men of high estate,
'Tis not the wealthy and the great,
But those your rights who advocate,
    Whose labours you do appreciate :
Let sons of toil unite to sing,
And each their humble tribute bring,
To cheer the heart of their old tried King,
    The King of the Factory Children.

THE WEALTHY
FARMER'S SON.

Come all ye pretty maidens fair, attend unto my song,
While I relate a story that does to love belong,
'Tis of a blooming damsel walking through the fields so gay,
And there she met her lover, who thus to her did say :—

Where are you going, young Nancy, this morning so gay,
Or why do you walk here alone ? come tell me I pray ?
I'm going to yon river's side that's just below the hill,
For to gather sweet flowers, and watch the fishes swim.

Be not in haste, dear Nancy, this young man he did say,
And I will bear you company, and guard you by the way,
For I live by yonder river's side, where fishes they do swim,
There you may gather flowers that grow around the brim.

Kind sir, you must excuse me, this maiden she did reply,
I'll ne'er walk with any man, until the day we die;
I have a sweetheart of my own, and he my heart has won,
He lives in yonder cottage, a wealthy farmer's son.

O then, replies this young man, tell me your lovers name,
Though in my tarry trousers perhaps I know the same,
Says she his name is William, from that I ne'er will run,
The ring he broke at parting, the wealthy farmer's son.

The ring then from his pocket instantly he drew,
Saying, Nancy, here's the parting gift, one half I left with you,
Oh, I have been press'd to sea and every battle won,
Yet still your heart could ne'er depart from me, the farmer's son.

O when these words she heard him say, he put her in surprise,
The tears they came fast tickling down from her sparkling eyes,
O sooth your grief the young man cries, the battle you have won,
For Hymen's chains shall bind you and the farmer's son.

To church then this couple went, and married were with speed,
The village bells they all did ring, and girls did dance indeed,
She bless'd that happy hour she in the fields did run,
To seek for her true lover the wealthy farmer's son.

Sold by W. Midgley, Bookseller, Russell Street, Halifax.

PLATE No. 17

HYMNS, TO BE SUNG

AT THE

SHEFFIELD AND BARNSLEY
CHARTIST CAMP-MEETING,

On Sunday, Sep. 22nd, 1839.

HYMN I.

*The following beautiful Composition was
written expressly for this occasion, by that
Philanthropic Friend of the People,*

E. ELLIOTT ESQ.

When Stewart reign'd, God's people fled,
Chased like the helpless hunted hare ;
But kneeling on the mountain's head,
There sought the Lord, and found him there.

Lord ! we, too, suffer ; we, too, pray,
That thou wilt guide our steps aright ;
And bless *this day,* tir'd labour's day !
And fill our souls with heavenly light.

For failing food, six days in seven,
We till the black town's dust and gloom ;
But *here* we drink the breath of heaven ;
And here, to pray the poor have room.

We seek the dewy, daisied plain,
Or climb thy hills, to touch thy feet ;
There, far from splendor's heartless fane,
Thy weary sons and daughters meet.

Where, wheeling wide, the plover flies
O'er field, and flood, and rock and tree ;
Beneath the silence of thy skies,
Is it a crime to worship thee ?

" We waited long, and sought thee Lord "
Content to toil, but not to pine ;
And with the weapons of thy word,
Alone assail'd, our foes and thine.

Thy truth and thee, we bade them fear ;
They spurn thy truth, and mock our moan !
" Thy counsels, Lord, they will not hear,
And thou hast left them to their own." •

• See the hymn of Rebecca, in Scott's Ivanhoe.

HYMN II.

Sad oppression now compels,
Working men to join themselves ;
Ye sufferers don't no more delay,
Work with might while it is day.
        CHORUS.
    I a Chartist now will be,
    And contend for liberty.

The Charter springs from Zion's hill,
Though opposed, go on it will ;
Will you serve its sacred cause,
And receive its equal laws.
        CHORUS.
    Union is our Captain's name,
    By just laws he'll rule the main ; ,
    Before his face he'll make to flee,
    All bad laws of tyranny.
        CHORUS.
    Brothers and sisters now unite,
    And contend for your just rights ;
    Then soon the poor will happy be,
    Glorious times we all shall see.
        And the Chartist's song shall be,
        My country and sweet liberty.

HYMN III.

Lord of all Lords, even Lord of they
Who claim us as their lawful prey ;
Who puff'd up high with lordly pride,
Thy poor despise, thy law deride.

Yea there are men in higher spheres,
Who mock our prayers, insult our tears ;
Great God, convince their haughty clay,
Thou made us men the same as they.

Teach them that we have hearts and arms,
Hearts—that the voice of friendship warms ;
Arms—that no nobler pleasures know,
Than to embrace a friend, or curb a foe.

Lord let them know that us oppose,
We wish to mend, not break the laws ;
Yet we can not from murmuring cease,
Till justice shall have purchas'd peace.

O let each manly bosom feel,
The glow of patriotic zeal ;
Strengthen'd with knowledge, arm'd with might,
To know and to assert our right.

The malice of our foes defeat,
Drive bigots from the judgement seat ;
And give us power to rend in twain
Each hateful link in slavery's chain.

                            A. S. G.

HYMN IV.

" When Adam delved and Eve span,
Who was then the gentleman ?"
        Wretched is the infant's lot,
        Born within the poor man's cot ;
Be he generous, wise, or brave,
He must only be a slave,
Long, long labour, little rest,
Still to toil to be oppressed ;
Drained by taxes of his store,
Punished next for being poor ;
This is the poor wretch's lot,
Born within the poor man's cot.
While the peasant works, to sleep—
What the peasant sows, to reap—
On the couch of ease to lie,
Rioting in revelry ;
Be he villain, be he fool,
Still to hold despotic rule ;
        Trampling on his slaves with scorn !
        This is to be nobly born.
" When Adam delved and Eve span,
Who was then the gentleman ?"

                            R. SOUTHEY ESQ.

O Lord our God arise,
Scatter our enemies,
        And make them fall ;
Confound their politics,
Frustrate their knavish tricks,
On thee our hopes we fix,
        God save us all.

E. SMITH, PRINTER, FARGATE.

AN HONEST MAN'S THE

NOBLEST WORK OF GOD.

The following *POETICAL LINES* were Printed by desire of the
SHEFFIELD COUNCIL OF THE NATIONAL CHARTER ASSOCIATION,
as a tribute of respect to the Memory of our departed Brother—

MR. THOMAS BRIGGS,

Who was Treasurer for the above Association upwards of Seven Years.

YES! honest BRIGGS hath breathed his last,
 His earthly sun hath set ;
The toils and cares of life are past,
 And paid is Nature's debt.

Mourn, Freedom, mourn, the hapless doom
 Which hurried him away,
To be a tenant of the tomb
 In life's meridian day.

See ! bending o'er the silent bier,
 His sorrowing Widow stand ;—
His Daughters, whom he loved so dear,
 Clasping his cold, cold hand.

But, vain their grief, for in *one* day
 His shattered reason fled !
The spoiler seized the hapless prey,
 And lowly laid his head.

Cut down, while hope was in its prime,
 As 'twere, in one short hour;
Swift borne beyond the stage of Time,
 By Death's resistless power.

The Poor have lost a generous friend,
 In whom they could confide ;
Their cause he studied to defend,
 And oft their wants supplied.

Let not the tongue of slander dare
 E'er trifle with his name !
Or malice spread her envious snare,
 His honour to defame !

He courted not the world's applause—
 His actions were sincere ;
His soul was wrapt in Freedom's cause,
 Which cost him many a tear.

Nor was it simple fame he sought—
 His thoughts were pure and free;
With heart and voice he nobly fought,
 For Right and Liberty !

Though humble, yet, 'tis well to know,
 Since busy life began,
To rich and poor, to friend and foe,
 He was at heart—a MAN !

Such honest worth demands a sigh,
 From every throbbing breast ;—
A pitying tear from every eye,
 A hope that he is blest.

Sheffield.   T. W. KING.

☞ *The above Verses were written, and kindly presented to the Chartist Body, by Mr. T. King, at the time*
of Mr. Briggs' Death, June 24th, 1848.

W. FORD, TYP.,]   [YORK STREET.

PRICE ONE PENNY.

PLATE No. 19

10 Quires
March 31st 1831.

Crown—3 on a
Sheet.

31 march 1831

First DREST MAN of SEGHILL,

Or the Pitman's Reward for Betraying his Brethren.—A New Song.

COME, all ye Miners, far and near,
    And let us all unite, o,
In bands of love and unity,
    And stand out for our right, o.
Like Israel, these many years,
    In bondage we have been, o ;
And if we do not still stand out
    Our truth will not be seen, o.
        With my fal lal la, &c.

No doubt but there may be some men
    Not bad for to deceive ;
But to their ruin it will be,
    Just like our mother Eve.
Our mother Eve was sore deceiv'd
    By one that's call'd the Devil ;
And by persuasion she was brought
    To do the thing that's evil.
Man a weak frail being ;
    And easy to deceive ;
And by a man call'd black J R.
    Was made for to believe—
It was on March the 19th. day,
    Eighteen hundred and thirty one,
A man from Earsdon Colliery
    His brethren did abscond.
And to the Seghill binding he
    Did come with all his might,
For to deceive his brethren dear,
    He thought he was but right.
But when he came to Seghill town
    The men were standing off ;
He thought that he would then be
        bound,
    And he would make a scoff.
As other men were standing off,
    He would not do the same ;
That idle work would never do,
    He'd rather bear the shame.
Black J. R. made him believe
    That he was in no danger,
And to the office he might go,
    Because he was a stranger.
He to the Seghill office went,
    All with a bad intent ;
But ere he got to Murton town
    He was made to lament.
He to the office went with speed,
    As hard as he could batter,
And other two young lads with him—
    We did give him a tatter.
Black J. R. made him believe
    That men would not molest ;
He being acquainted with the man
    He was with faith possest.
We kept the fugal-man in view,
    Which made us all so keen ;
For it's an oath, by brethren all,
    No one they are to screen.
We went in chace of this bad man,
    For to give him a scar—
By coming to our bond, you know,
    To serve the man J. R.

And at the hour of two o'clock,
    As I was sitting cobbling,
A rout there came unto our house,
    I heard the women gabbling.
Away I went with all my speed,
    As hard as I could hie,
To see if I could catch the hares—
    It was my will to try.
We gladly found him at the pit,
    With J. R. and G. Sern ;
But our hearts were fully bent,
    Not to stand there bothering.
But there were some upon the chace
    Long ere I got there :
With running so I lost my breath,
    And I could run ne mair.
But I will tell his travels here,
    As he went from the binding ;
They stript him there of part his
        clothes,
    And left his skin resining.
Black J R. was all the blame,
    He lost all but his lining :
But when he came to Hallowell
    His skin so bright was shining.
They left him nothing on to hide
    The good old man the, priest.
But there they put him on his hat,
    He was so finely drest.
They set him off from there with speed
    To an ale-house by the way ;
And there the Earsdon men did sit,
    A drinking on that day.
But what their minds I cannot tell,
    When they did see him coming ,
The priest he had within his hat,
    And hard he then was running.
And all the way as he went home,
    By many was heard say,
That persuaded he had been
    To his loss upon that day.
The Earsdon men they set him off
    From there to the Machine,
That stands upon the allotment hill ;
    He there himself did screen.
Then to the left hand road he took,
    The road that leads to Murton,
And there under a good whin bush
    The priest and him sat lurking.
The priest was almost starved there—
    I'm afraid he has got harm,
If I was only into bed
    I quickly shall be warm.
But unto Paradise I'll go,
    Where I will get no ill,
But never more will I go back
    To that place call'd Seghill.
But remember you that come
    Unto Seghill to bind,
You may think upon the man
    That we have treat so kind.

J. Marshall, Printer, Newcastle.

THE
PITMEN'S
AGREEMENT

A NEW SONG.

Written in Commemoration of a great Number
of them gaining their Rights, after a very
long Contention with the Coal-Owners, in
the Year 1831.

COME all you honest pitmen lads,
   And listen a short while ;
It is concerning the agreement,
   Your time I will beguile.

A glorious victory you have gain'd
   Over your stubborn foes,
(Makes me sing these lines with glee)
   Which every body knows.

Some of you have been badly used,
   Most shamefully used indeed ;
For out of doors you have been turn'd,
   And left you without bread.

Some of you have been turn'd out of doors,
   Which I do still maintain,
Complying not with the demands of those,
   Whose house you did retain.

During the whole of your manly strike,
   Your conduct have been brave—
Which deserves the country's thanks,
   And the nation's praise.

All those men that are not bound
   Cheer up your daring hearts—
Patience and Perseverance, my lads,
   Be still your nobler parts.

Should you any act of violence commit,
   A stigma on you will be ;
The military force will interfere,
   Which you will plainly see.

All those men that have got bound,
   For their aid you must call,
To give you part of their earnings,
   For fear that you should fall.

After you have all agreed, my lads,
   (I hope you'll excuse my rhyme)
In a sacred bond join heart and hand,
   To support you 'nother time.

Now success to all the pitmen,
   Both on the Tyne and Wear ;
May they continue to have their rights
   In each succeeding year.

Success attend their canny wives,
   And all their children dear,
Forgetting not the Delegates,
   Who had the cause to steer.

Douglas and Kent, Printers, Newcastle.

PLATE No. 21

PETERLOO

Harkness, Printer, Church Street, Preston.

See! see! where Freedom's noblest champion
   stands,
Shout! shout! illustrious patriot band,
Here grateful millions their generous tribute
   bring,
And shouts for freedom make the welkin ring,
While fell corruption and her hellish crew,
The blood stain'd trophies gain'd at Peterloo.

Soon shall fair freedom's sons their right regain,
Soon shall all Europe join the hallowed strain,
Of Liberty & Freedom, Equal Rights & Laws,
Heaven's choisest blessings crown this glorious
   cause,
While meanly, tyrants, crawling minions too,
Tremble at their feats performed on Peterloo.

Britons be firm, assert your rights, be bold,
Perish like heroes, not like slaves be sold,
Firm and unite, bid millions be free,
Will to your children glorious liberty.
While cowards—despots, long may keep in view
And silent contemplate, the deeds on Peterloo.

PLATE NO. 22

The New Starvation Law examined,

And some Description of the Food, Dress, Labour, and Regulations, imposed upon the poor and unfortunate Sufferers in the New British Bastiles.

Come you men and women unto me attend,
And listen and see what for you I have penn'd;
And if you do buy it, and carefully read,
'T will make your hearts within you to bleed.

The lions at London, with their cruel paw,
You know they have pass'd a Starvation Law;
These tigers and wolves should be chained in a den,
Without power to worry poor women and men.

Like the fox in the farm-yard they shly do creep;
These hard-hearted wretches, O, how dare they sleep,
To think they should pass such a law in our day,
To bate and to stop the poor widow's pay.

And if they don't like their pay to be stopp'd,
'Gainst their own will into th' Bastile they're popp'd;
Their homes must break up, and never return,
But leave their relations and children to mourn.

The three pension'd paupers in grandeur do live,
Pon riches that they from the taxes receive;
Which poor people pay from their scanty week's wage,
Though pinch'd, and confin'd like a bird in a cage.

But if they'd to work before they were fed,
They'd not go a tolling the poor children's bread,
Which fathers do earn very hard every day,
While they in carriages are dashing away.

There's many poor children go ragged and torn,
While they and their horses are pamper'd with corn;
Now is not this world quite unequally dealt?
The Starvation Law by some few is felt.

When a man and his wife for sixty long years
Have toiled together through troubles and fears,
And brought up a family with prudence and care,
To be sent to the Bastile it's very unfair.

And in the Bastile each woman and man
Is parted asunder,—is this a good plan?
A word of sweet comfort they cannot express,
For unto each other they ne'er have access.

Of their uniform, too, you something shall bear,—
In strong Fearnaught jackets the men do appear;
In coarse Grogram gowns the women do shine,
And a ninepenny cap,—now won't they be fine?

On fifteenpence halfpenny they keep them a week;
Had Commissioners this we should have them to seek,
They'd not come to Yorkshire to visit us here,
And of such vile vermin we soon should be clear.

To give them hard labour, it is understood,
In handmills the grain they must grind for their food,
Like men in a prison they work them in gangs,
With turning and twining it fills them with pangs.

I'll give you an insight of their regulations,
Which they put in force in these situations,
They've school, chapel, and prison all under a roof,
And the governor's house stands a little aloof.

The master instructs them the law to obey,
The governor minds it's all work and no play,
And as for religion the parson doth teach
That he knows the gospel,—no other must preach.

Ye hard-working men, wherever you be,
I'd have you watch closely these men, d'ye see;
I think they're contriving, the country all o'er,
To see what's the worst they can do to the poor.

But if that their incomes you wish for to touch,
They'll vapour, and grumble, and talk very much,
The Corn Laws uphold, the poor will oppress,
And send them to th' Bastile in th' day of distress.

R. H.

PLATE No. 23

A DIALOGUE

Between Harry Heartless and Peter Pluck.

P. Good mornin Harry, how dis things luk now ?
    A good way better than when aw saw thou,
    But yet aw guess, by that grave luk o' thine,
    Thou still dost murmer, and dost still repine,
    Aw really dinna understand sic folks ;
    Ye're only easy under Tyrant's yokes,
    Freedom charms ye not, an if it only cost,
    A single hungry belly, 'twad be lost.

H. Nay Peter, thou's harder than thou ought to be,
    A coward aw never was, nor thought to be ;
    But still if aw mun tell thee all my mind,
    How things should better luk aw canna find :
    The Maisters still are stiff, an men most dune,
    An blacklegs at wark—the fight's not yet won.

P. Nut won ! that aw'l awn, but it's nut lost,
    It may last a few days, or a few weeks at most,
    An as for the blacklegs thou's talkin about,
    Not being in the Union, they could'nt come out.
    But what use are they te, the spiritless villains !
    If they'll swap us price, we'll mak punds for their shillins,
    An the few coals they hew are all mix'd wi' dirt,
    Yet they're dear as the best, man, keep up thy heart.
    The Maisters are stiff, aye as stiff as a prop,
    But props sometimes crack, when the stone starts to drop.
    And the Maisters though stiff will bend before lang,
    An when it dis cum it will come in a bang.

H. Wey Peter thou luks at it different fra me,
    A bright side o' the question aw wad like te see,
    But the viewers and shopkeepers all seem to 'gree,
    To stop the bit credit, then what can we de ?
    The straingers aw's flaid 'll come down fra the south,
    An tak the bit bread that we hev fra our mouth,
    When there's just grund te hope man aw can hope,
    But now aw see nane, an we'd better give up.

P. Give up, Harry ! never, as lang as there's reason
    To hope we can win, an it's not yet the season,
    To groan and despair, t' winge and to yield,
    It is'nt lost yet an we'll still keep the field.
    The Maisters are quakin, but wear a good face,
    To be rogues and luck rogues wad be a disgrace,
    What less can they de ? it's nought but a fudge,
    And aw wonder Harry thou's sic a bad judge.
    Thou kens 's weel as me at the last greet lang strike,
    The Maister's behaviour was just the same like,
    Ane thief the ——— aw'l not tell his name,
    He said to the men they might all be gaun hame,
    For what they were axin he never wad pay,
    They got all they ax'd for the very next day.
    'Tis true the shopkeepers hae stopt the bit cridit,
    But stop a short while an they'll rue that they dit it,
    We may yet win the day, then they're properly drawn,
    'When we get baith shopkeepers and shops o' our awn,
    Then let's keep our hearts up and help ane another,
    An in every Unionest luk at a brother.

H It's very strange Peter ne odds what it be,
    About which we differ, we're sure t'gree,
    Yet thou never flinches it's sure to be me,
    Thou sees things se ready an niver a stammer,
    Ane wad swear thou had studied baith logic aa grammer.
    A'l e'en tak thy advice and keep up my heart,
    An niver till we get what we want will au start.

P. That's reet Harry lad, we'll not flinch a peg,
    We'll eat what we hev, an then start an beg,
    We'll tell them plain stories what we hev felt,
    For experience tells better than ony that's telt,
    We'll tell a' the fines, a' the set-out, an laid-out,
    O' the doctor, an house rent, an other things paid out,
    O' the trifles that's left to get meat for our wives,
    'Wor bairns an 'worsels to keep in 'wor lives,
    An aw ken when they hear us, they'll give us their aid,
    An help us to equal the other men of trade.

COMPOSED SOLELY FOR THE BENEFIT OF THE

Men of Framwellgate Moor Colliery,

By one of Themselves.

PLATE No. 24

A NEW SONG.

TUNE—"Auld lang syne."

How, Jobson, has the heard the news
   About this d——d wire rope—
That Durham men (they mun be Jews)
   Hev left us nowt to hope.
     Maw wife sal darn and cloot maw claise,
       An brush maw Sunday coat ;
     An ne mair unyen au me days,
       Or thou sal cut me throte.

Our delegats are nowt but theves ;
   They've rob'd us au thegether.
We've pan'd our beds, and best sark sleves,
   Wor byuts of guid caff' lether
     Maw wife, &c.

Our wives an bairns ha nowt to eat,
   This twenty weeks, an mair ;
We ha ne tyeble, nor ne meet ;
   A man, that's vara sair.
     Maw wife, &c.

This *Rob* we may sa's ful o' *arts,*
   And B——y just as bad ;
We now see through their roguish parts ;
   Wy man, we've au been mad
     Maw wife, &c.

We thowt him just the king o' harts,
   See clever an see brave ;
Now see how he wor cause desarts,
   An hes turned out pick nave.
     Maw wife, &c.

There's only ane thing noo, aw hope,
   An wish it from my heart,—
That R——s was hung in a rope
   And B——y had his part.
     Maw wife, &c.

They've left us bare o' bed and claes—
   De'il brust them every yen—
Wi thare deceitful leein ways
   They've left us siller—nyen.
     Maw wife, &c.

Aw ken what's the furst thing aw dees,—
   Aw'll just gan to maw wark,
To get the bairns some breed a chees
   Aw'll strip inte me sark.
     Maw wife, &c.

May R——s, B——y gan to h—l,
   The unyen to the de'il,
Maw wife an bairns agyen live well
   On wheet and haver meal.
     Maw wife, &c-

Now sharp maw picks, and trim maw lamp,
   Maw hoggars, an pit shun—
Aw'll through the country ne mair tramp
   Until maw life be duin.
     Maw wife, &c.

Now mine me, pit lads, yen an au,
   Ne mair wi hungry guts—
Maw Jack sal to the huin fa,
   An Tommy fills and puts.
     Maw wife sal darn and cloot me claes,
       An brush my Sunday coat ;
     And ne mair unyen au me days,
       Or thou sal cut me throte.

Printed by J. PROCTER, Hartlepool.

PLATE No. 25

SOUTH YORKSHIRE LOCK-OUT.

Barnsley Collieries.

Just in the dawn of youth we stand,
The hope and promise of our land,
From custom's yoke we turn away,
Resolved, resolved, to win the day.

Rebellion, riots, lay them down,
They ruin cities, countries, towns,
We show to you a better way,
In which we're sure to win the day.

We do believe these time are sent
For warning and for punishment,
But ports are open all to say
There we may trade and win the day.

May every miner soon be free
From bondage and from misery;
Forsake our sins without delay,
Press on and we shall win the day.

And though the conflict be severe,
And we have many trials here,
We'll never mind, but gladly say,
We mean, we mean, to win the day.

Give what you please.

PLATE NO. 26

The Great Lock-out
OF
Miners
AT BARNSLEY.

NEW SONG:
"The South Yorkshire Miners shall Never Despair."

Tune—Nil Desperandum.

Kind Sons of Old England pray listen awhile,
　We are all "Lock-outs" in great distress,
We have lately travelled many a mile,
　Yet trouble and care have grown no less;
But whatever our lot, 'mid hunger and care,
Sing "The South Yorkshire Miners shall never despair."

We're fighting for rights, that are justly our due
　For the dangers we all undergo,—
Give the workman fair-play, then no one will rue
　That he claimed what was right, I know.
So brave every trial and ev'ry care,
For "The South Yorkshire Miners shall never despair."

At last, when this troublesome Lock-out is o'er,
　And our children have plenty of bread,
We then shall remember our true friends of yore,
　Who kindly supported us, and said
Stick up for your rights, lads, and have what is fair,
For, "The South Yorkshire Miners shall never despair."

A fair day's wage for a fair day's work.

These Sheets are Sold to MINERS ONLY, at Whitham's, New Street

PLATE NO. 27

The Barnsley Miners' Lock-out.

MASTER, be honoured as Master should,
Workman be honoured as Workmen should,
Laws and Regulations soundly made,
Not to destroy, but to establish trade.

THE Master and the public say
The trade has left the land ;
Both coal and wages must come down
If not, the works must stand.

They tell us very plainly too
They mean to use their powers,
In bringing us poor miners back
To slavery and long hours.

The law to regulate the Mines
The masters all declare ;
Has thrown them to so much expense
It leaves no gold to share.

Each firm must have a manager,
Dwelling on the ground,
With Government certificate—
This takes a thousand pounds.

Then there's the mining engineer,
His duties I can't tell,
He takes another thousand pounds—
I think that's pretty well.

Some firms keep two directors,
Each costs a thousand pounds ;
They too must have a country seat,
With park and pleasure grounds.

Then there's the board of intellect,
This takes a thousand more ;
Such times they say were never seen
In Barnsley before.

Next comes the Clerk, that keeps the books
He gets four hundred pounds,
Because he goes three days a week
A hunting with the hounds.

Each firm must keep a good Cashier,
He too must have good pay,
Because the cash goes through his hands
Before it's paid away.

Next comes the Lawyer with his wit
A clever man they say ;
He advocates the masters' cause,
And don't he make them pay !

These are the men that advocate
Reductions for each man,
But don't forget to raise themselves
As often as they can.

The cost of all this management,
They never will expose,
Nor publish through the publc press
Which way the money goes.

But as reductions come again,
I feel in duty bound,
To ask that those should be reduced
Who get their thousand pounds.

If coal and wages must come down,
I think it only fair,
That every one receiving wage,
Should be reduced his share.

Now if the public this should see,
My labour wont be lost,
If I have shown why coal is dear,
By showing them the cost.

If this should meet a Master's eye,
While looking o'er the news,
I hope he'll never show his spite,
Nor the rhyming one abuse.

We are poor Barnsley miners,
Standing for our rights,
We hope you all will help us,
By giving us your mite.

PLATE No. 28

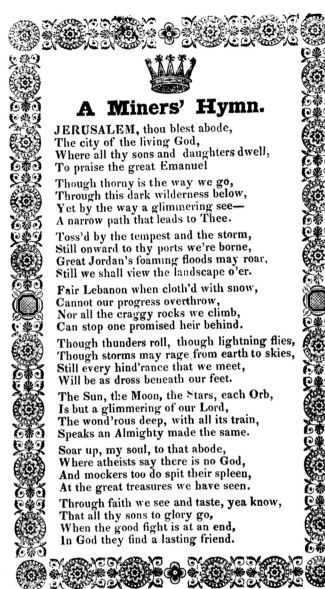

A Miners' Hymn.

JERUSALEM, thou blest abode,
The city of the living God,
Where all thy sons and daughters dwell,
To praise the great Emanuel

Though thorny is the way we go,
Through this dark wilderness below,
Yet by the way a glimmering see—
A narrow path that leads to Thee.

Toss'd by the tempest and the storm,
Still onward to thy ports we're borne,
Great Jordan's foaming floods may roar,
Still we shall view the landscape o'er.

Fair Lebanon when cloth'd with snow,
Cannot our progress overthrow,
Nor all the craggy rocks we climb,
Can stop one promised heir behind.

Though thunders roll, though lightning flies,
Though storms may rage from earth to skies,
Still every hind'rance that we meet,
Will be as dross beneath our feet.

The Sun, the Moon, the Stars, each Orb,
Is but a glimmering of our Lord,
The wond'rous deep, with all its train,
Speaks an Almighty made the same.

Soar up, my soul, to that abode,
Where atheists say there is no God,
And mockers too do spit their spleen,
At the great treasures we have seen.

Through faith we see and taste, yea know,
That all thy sons to glory go,
When the good fight is at an end,
In God they find a lasting friend.

JOHN ELLIOTT, PRINTER, BARNSLEY.

TO  THE
PUBLIC.

The Ship-builders of the Tyne having stated in a Hand-bill that they had taken it into Consideration to Employ 150 Ship-wrights, (out of 700 unemployed,) at 21s. per Week in consequence of the great Distress prevailing in the Neighbourhood, (and Sunderland in particular,) we, the Ship-wrights of the Tyne, are ready to serve any Ship-builder at the aforesaid Wages, either for six, eight or twelve Months but we would wish to intimate to the Public that we have been accosted by Mr. Mc'Leod, the Agent for the Middle Dock Company, and Mr. James Edwards to work for 21s. per Week, but instead of 21s. per Week it proves to be 3s. 6d. per Day; now for the last twelve Months we have been working for 4s. per Day, and our average Wages per Week for the best employed Men in the River, has not exceeded 14s. 7d. per Week, and for the second best employed, not more than 9s. 5d. per Week, and for the worst part not more than 6s. 4d. per Week; now we would leave it to the better Judgment of the Public, to ascertain what might be our average Wages at 3s. 6d. per Day, when we, the Ship-wrights of the Tyne have given our average Wages per Week, at 4s. per Day, and we would wish to inform the Public that Mr. Metcalfe intimated to us for a Reduction of Wages, and he told us that if the Men would go to work for 1s. per Day, Mr. Forsyth either would not or could not employ one Man; yet the time may come when we will have an opportunity to raise our Wages, then the Ship-owners of the Tyne may thank Mr Mc'Leod, Mr. Smith, and Mr. Edwards, for the high rate of Wages paid in the Tyne.

South Shields, 4th August, 1842.

Market Place Printing Offices: R. M. Kelly, South Shields.

A NEW SONG
ON
THE TURN-OUT.

Hurra for every sporting blade,
Of Liverpool and Birkenhead,
That will support the strike in trade,
   Against the Master Builders;
Let every man now well agree,
United in society,
The banners of sweet liberty,
   Will crown your cause most glorious,
           Hurrah, &c,

The master men are not content,
Unless that you will give consent,
To sign a binding document,
   Against the law of nature.
Why should you rob your family,
And drive yourselves to misery,
To yield unto their tyranny,
   Of silly Master Builders.

In order for to put you down,
Two masters went to London town,
To get assistance from the crown,
   They spoke to Sir James Graham.
Their journey it was all in vain,
Altho' they went upon the train,
They're turning light all in the brain,
   The strike will soon be ended.

You bricklayers and you masons all,
You Carpenters both great and small,
Be firm and do not shrink at all,
   Unto the Master Builders;
The Master Builders in a squad,
Will dance to the tune of Moll-in-the-
   Wad,
The gallant men that carry the hod,
   Does cry out no surrender.

See Scotland's sons, as brave as Bruce,'
As wild as tigers when let loose,
Does cry against the great abuse,
   Of silly Master Builders;
For while one penny's in the funds,
And boxes will be over-runn'd,
The Master Builders will be stunn'd,
   To see the trades in union.

That silly elf they call S. H——s,
Will shortly have to go break stones,
Or else go gather rags and bones,
   For toffy in the morning.
His buildings are going to decay,
Before the 21st of May,
Unto the strike he must give way,
   like men be well united.

Now Mr T———n how do you do,
I am none the better of seeing you,
You've got me in a pretty stew,
   My buildings are all idle,
I have much reason for to fret,
I never will be out of debt,
The strike I never will forgot,
   You silly Sammy sly boots.

So to conclude and make an end,
Success attend each loyal friend,
That will a hand to freedom lend,
   To crush Monopoly;
Be firm, undaunted, loyal and true,
The Master Builders you'll subdue,
They are beginning to look blue,
   The tyranizing creatures.

Mc. Call, printer, 81, Cheapside,
Liverpool.

SOLD HERE,
CORVAN'S
Popular Songs.

1 Warkworth Feast.
2 Toon Improvement; or, Ne pleyce to Play.
3 Sandgate Lass.
4 Rise i' Coals.
5 Pitman an' Kipper'd Herrin'.
6 A'strilly; or, the Pitman's Fareweel.
7 Keel on Fire, a parody on the ship on Fire.
8 Stage Struck Keelman.
9 Bonny Bella Gray.
10 Astrilly's Goold Fields; or Tommy Carr's Letter
11 Unfortunate Man.
12 Pally Jones the Factory Lass.
13 Swagerin' at the Races.
14 He wad be a Noodle,
15 Trip to Marsden Rock.
16 Maw Stepmother; or, Billy Baggs the Glutton.
17 In the Days when I was Hard Up.
18 Hairy Gobs; or, New Moosecatchers.
19 Deeth o' Billy Purvis.
20 The Queen's Second Visit; or, the Openin' o' wor
   Greet Central Station-
21 Prince Albert's Babby Hoose; or the Greet Exhi-
   bition for 1851.
22 Cullercoats Fishwife.

Also,
J. P. ROBSON'S

Landin' o' the Frenchers   Cod Liver Oil.
Horrid War i' Sangeyt.   And

Robert Emery's
Deeth o' Bobby Nunn.
And Deeth o' Billy Purvis.

Together with nearly Ten Thousand Local and other
Comic and Sentimental Songs,

Published by W. STEWART, Head of the Side, New-
castle-on-Tyne; and may be had of J. Gilbert, Royal
Arcade; Bagnall, Nun-St; Everat, Newgate-St.;
Mitford, corner of High Bridge, Bigg Market; Har-
rison, Murray, and others, Green Market; P. France
and Co, Side, Newcast'e; Stewart, Botchergate, Car-
lisle; Hodgson, Fore-St., Hexham; Bunn, Waterloo
Vale, South Shields; and of E. Corvan, 16, Covent
Garden, Sunderland.

CORVAN AS "CAT-GUT JIM."

PLATE NO. 31

THE
TOON IMPROVEMENT BILL;

OR, NEE PLEYCE NOO TO PLAY.

An Original Song written by Edward Corven, and Sung by him with immense applause at the Royal Olympic Music Hall, Newcastle

---

AIR.—"Na Luck about the House."

Noo, O dear me, what mun aw dee, aw've nee playce noo ti play,
Wor canny Forth an' Spital tee, eh, man, they've teyne away.
Nee pleyce ti bool wos peyste eggs noo, ti lowp the frog or run ;
They're elways beeldin summuck new they'll spoil Newcastle seune.

SPOKEN.—Thors nee place ti play the wag noo ; the grund's a' tuen up wiv High Levels Central Stations, an' dear knaws what else. Aw used ti play the wag doon the quay thonder Aw've seen me fish for days tigither. The lads ca'd me the fisherwoman's boy. Aw was a stunner. Aw've monny a time browt up three rotten French apples at a time ; but wor auld wife said if aw fell in an' gat droon'd she'd skin me alive when aw com heyme ; so aw play-ed the wag doon the burn efter that, but noo ti meyke improvements they've filled it up wi' cairt loads o' muck, to beeld hooses on ; some o' wor lads an' me petitioned the magistrators for a new play grund, an' he tell'd us ti gan ti boardin schuels. What an idia. Wor auld wife hes sair tues ti raise the penny for Monday mornins, the maister seldom gets't though, aw buy claggum wid, then the maister hes ti teyke't oot i' flaps. But aw's broken hearted when aw think aboot wor canny Forth wiv its auld brick wall ; what curious days aw've spent there ; man, aw've seen me play the wag for heyle days tigither, wi' maw mooth cover'd all ower wi' claggum an' clarts. What a chep aw was for one-hole-teazer then ; monny a time aw've fowt an hoor for a farden bullocker ; aw used ti skin thor knockles when aw won me beeks ; aw used ti fullock, man what a fullocker aw was. But what's the use o' jawin' noo, the auld gams is a' geyne. Thors widdy-widdy-way, the morrow's the market day, sly-ater, slyater, comin' away, comin' away ; an' king Henry's boys go roond, what a gam that was : av used ti be king Henry. But aw'd better drop off or else maw feelin's 'ill set me on a bubblin', for

O dear me what mun aw dee, aw've nee pleyce noo to play,
Wor canny Forth an' Spital tee, eh, man, they've tuene away.

The toon improvement's meyde greet noise, but aw heard my feyther say,
Thor was summick mair than little boys kept wor wise heeds at play ;
There's bonny wark amang thorsels, but aw mun haud maw jaw ;
But still thors folks 'boot here that smells the cash buik wiv its flaws.

SPOKEN.—Aw heard my feyther tell maw muther, yen neet, all aboot the toon concerns they thought aw was asleep. Aw's a cute lad. Aw's elways wakcn when the tripe's fryin for feyther's supper ; aw heard him say thor was a vast o' rates, sic as poor rates, leet rates, sewer rates, an' watch rates ; but aw think, at onny rate, thor's nee first-rate rates amang them. Noo thor's the watch rate, that's the pollis, noo we cannit dee wivoot pollis, but it's not fair ti teyke a chep up for playin' at holes ; but the magistrates isn't deein fair wiv us at nowt. Aw's lossin a' maw lairnin' noo. What a heed-piece aw had yen time, aw'd ti use a shoe-horn ti put maw Sunday hat on, maw heed gat swelled wiv knowledge sac. noo a' thor days is geyne, so aw'll lairn ti chew bseey, etc., etc.

For O dear me, what mun aw de, aw've nee pleyce noo ti play,
Wor canny Forth an' Spital tee, eh, man, they've tuene away.

Bedstocks that canny gam's noo dune, an' three hole teazer tee ;
They've tuene away wor best o' fun, so, lads, what mun aw dee ;
Aw'll bubble tiv aw dee, begox, or teyke some arsynack ;
Then corporation men may funk, when aw's laid on maw back.
                    For O dear me, etc.

Noo a' ye canny folks that's here, just think on what aw say,
An' recollect yor youthful days, when ye were fond o' play.
Ye say yor schule days was the best, so help me in maw cause,
An' cheer poor Bobby Snivvelnose by gean him yor applause.
    For O dear me, what mun aw dee, aw've nee pleyce noo ti play,
    Wor canny Forth an' Spital tee, eh, man, they've tuene away.

COPYRIGHT.

No. 2.

PUBLIS   BY W. STEWART, HEAD OF THE SIDE,
    'WCASTLE-ON-TYNE.

PLATE No. 32

THE
FACTORY LASS
OR PALLY JONES.

An Original Song, by E. Corven.

Air,—"Sunny Banks of Scotland.

Aw's Pally Jones the factory lass, an' fairly worth a score ;
Maw feyther an' mother's keelmen, and we all leve doon the shore.
    O laddie, ho ! bonny on the door,
    For aw's Pally Jones the factory lass.

SPOKEN.—Aw work at the spinnin' mill, sometimes at the white lead factory, an'

    Aw leve doon on the shore.
    O laddie, ho ! bonny laddie, ho !

Oh ! maw mother's sic a canny body her mouth hads three penorth o' rum,
An' feyther likes his whiskey toddy, but aw like beer begum.
    O laddie, ho ! ye've niver saw me before,
    But aw's Pally Jones the factory lass,
    That leve's doon the shore.

An' Bobby Nunn, that's deed an' geyn, used to fiddle doon the shore,
Often said, he niver saw the yen could touch me on the floor.
                    O laddie, ho, etc.

New sixes, cast offs, sylphs an' reels, aw could de them a' like fun ;
Folks said aw was sae polkerfied, aw'd sic a bonny run.
                    O laddie, ho, etc.

Aw've set the men folks ravin' mad, thor's twe wants me to wed,
But aw've a canny blacksmith lad, folks call him bonny Ned.
                    O laddie, ho, etc.

SPOKEN.—He hes nice curly hair ; an' sic nice ways wi' him. He's ganin t' hev me, an' aw's ganin t' hev him, so we'll set up hoose efter we get married. Aw say, which finger dis the ring gan on. Aw sure it meyks me feel queer when aw think on't ; but noo for settin' up house, let me see, O aye, aw'll hev a feather bed i' the first place, wi' pillow heed an' foot, so as we can lie heeds t' tails if ony friends should com' to stop a day or se. Aw'll buy a coffee mill, and maek maw man grind the coffee—coffee beans, that's the sort. Aw'll hev flour pots, tea pot, sugar pots, milk pots, keyle pots, an' —— chamber pots. Aw'll hev an oil cloth, an' put a pattern on't mysel' ; an' thou knaws we might hae bairns, so when aw is buyin' aw may as weel just buy a cradle, an' then when aw's rockin' the bairn to sleep aw'll sing

    O laddie, ho ! bonny on the door,
    For aw's Pally Jones the factory lass.

12.   COPYRIGHT.

Published by W. STEWART, Head of the Side, Newcastle.

PLATE No. 33

PRICE ONE HALFPENNY.

THE GREET STRIKE;

OR, THE NINE OORS MOVEMENT.

Noo, Tom, maw man, it's nine days noo
  Since ye turned oot on strike,
So, efter this short tyest we've had,
  Just let's see what it's like :
Then forst of awl, on Friday neet
  No wages ye browt hyem ;
But as wor teeth ar'n't oot on strike,
  We'd awl te eat the syem.

So awl last week we leeved upon
  Pooer Tommy's new Race sewt ;
An' what we pinched so sair te git,
  Pooer thing, he'll gan withoot.
An' noo, this week, we'll finish up
  The savins for yor hat ;
An' maw new dress, an' Jinny's, too,
  'Ill gan alang wi that.

Ye're strikin' for the nine oors, Tom—
  That aw'll say nowt agyen :
Nine oors may be eneuf te work,
  But noo ye're workin' nyen.
It's reet an' fair, by kwiet means,
  The nine oors for te win,
But strikin' for'd oot-hand at wouse,
  It's rang, lad, te begin.

Ye knaw, aw buy me shoos, me claes,
  Awl things aw yowse at hyem,
Just where aw get them cheepist at—
  An' uthors dis the syem :

An' if ye work but nine oors here,
  When uthors work the ten,
How can yor maistors get a job,
  An' pay thor nine oors' men ?

It mun begin sum place, ye say,
  That's true eneuf, aw see ;
But this nine oors, ye spoke on't forst
  Three weeks since, at yor tee.
Three weeks te tawk ower such a change !
  Three weeks te tawk awl clear !
Three 'ears ye mite hev tawkt it ower,
  An' spred it far an' near.

Last neet, aw bowt the " Hapny Xpress,"
  The letter for te see
George Robert Stivisin sent hees men,
  An' fair it seem'd te me :
It cleerly, fairly, kindly tell'd
  Hoo he stud wiv his men ;
An' they, like thowtfil, carefil foak
  Turn'd ti thor wark agyen.

Improvemints cum but slowly roond,
  Yit forsin dis but ill ;
The world wants much te put it reet,
  But time is workin' still :
An' time 'll bring yor nine oors yit,
  Wi' mair that's gud an' true ;
An' show te men an' maistors byeth
  The world 'll haud the two.

Published by T. Allan, Wholesale Bookseller, Stationer, and Newsagent, 62, Dean Street, and 16, Collingwood Street, Newcastle.

WE'LL SEUN HEH WARK TE DE !

OR, THE STRIKE O' '71.

WRITTEN BY

JOE WILSON,

And sung by him at the "Oxford" Music Hall, Newcastle,
received nightly with most tremendous applause.

TEUN—"NOWT TE DE."

"On Strike !" aw hear them awful words
Repeated i' the street,
"On strike ! ne wark !" aw hear agyen,
Frae hundreds that aw meet,
"Three lang munths gyen,—not sattled yit !
Wor hard-up as can be,
It cannet last, thor'll be a change,
We'll seun heh wark te de !"

KORUS.

Walkin roond the Market,
An' walkin doon the Kee,
The only cheerin words aw hear's
" We'll seun heh wark te de !"

Aw see the poor cheps oot on strike
Gan slawly throo the street,
Tho' anxshus for the latest news,
Frev iv'ry one they meet,
They keep up one-anuther's hearts,
As honest men shud be,
Wi' hopes the day's not distant when
They'll all heh wark te de !

" Mair forriners !" aw hear them say
Then one 'ill shake his heed—
" They may get plenty men as cheap,
But is't them that they need ?
No, no ! it's real mechanicks that
A maister likes te see,
Nine oors te him's a better thing,
Gud men his wark te de !"

" At hyem thor's nowt but misery,
Where happy days we've seen,
When plenty wark an' plenty keep
Myed a' things luck soreen,
We'll heh them gud things back agyen,
Seun settled we shall be,
Then forrin culls may tyek thor hook
Frae wark they cannet de !"

" We'll seun heh wark te de, me lads !
God bliss us a' we will,
Tyneside 'ill yit victorious shine,
Wi' men o' worth an' skill,
An' happier days 'ill myek the past
A dream o' what we see,
Men gud an' true 'ill nivor rue,
We'll seun heh wark te de !"

All JOE WILSON'S SONG BOOKS always on hand.

CHEAP BOOKS—GREAT CHOICE ! SCHOOL BOOKS—GREAT VARIETY !

Published by THOS. ALLEN, Bookseller,

62, DEAN STREET, & 16, COLLINGWOOD STREET, NEWCASTLE.

PLATE NO. 35

A STREET-MARKET ON SATURDAY NIGHT.

THE GIRLS
OF
Lancashire.

Attend you lads and lasses and a story you shall hear,
Concerning of the pretty girls that dwell in Lancashire,
Their cheeks are like roses they are comely gay and fair,
And there is no girls in England like the girls of Lancashire.

CHORUS

They are handsome they are charming & so comly they appear
Good temper'd, brisk, and lively, rosy cheeks as you near,
And the prettiest girls in England is the girls of Lancashire.

Through England, and Ireland, and Scotland I have been
And over the Welsh mountains where beauty I have seen,
But of all the lasses in the world I solemnly declare.
There is none that take my fancy like the girls of Lancashire,

There's Jane and Sal, and lovely Ann how cheerfully they jog
I often have admired them when dancing in their clogs,
Maria, and Eliza, and Ketty too so fair,
May happiness attend the pretty girls of Lancashire.

Some can brew and some can bake as you may plainly see,
And others weave beautifully while in the factory,
Some will tie a handkerchief around their pretty hair,
Sure you never saw such lasses as the girls of Lancashire.

Now many parts of Lancashire I make a solemn vow,
The lasses sing like nightingales when milking of the cows
And others dance a hornpipe at the races or a fair,
What charming blooming features have the girls of Lancashire

When I was down in Lancashire I heard a fair maid say,
Oh, John, false-hearted Johnny, you have stole my heart away
You have gone to court some other and quite forsaken me
And you left me little Johnny for to dandle on my knee.

Behold the farmer's daughter with their reticule and veil,
And a hairy thing tied round her neck just like a donkey's tail
Silk gloves, and dandy ribbons to tie up their lovely hair,
Oh the blooming farmer's daughters who reside in Lancashire.

You buxom blades of England if you wish to change your life
Come hasten into Lancashire and choose yourself a wife,
When you are tied in wedlock's bands a bumper fill to cheer,
And drink a health to the dancing blooming girls of Lancashire.

WITH
MY JUG
IN ONE HAND.

Harkness, Printer, 121, Church-street, Preston.

With my pipe in one hand, and my jug in
the other,
I drink to my neighbours and friend,
All my cares in a whiff of tobacco I smother,
For life I know shortly must end.

And while Ceres most kindly refills my
brown jug,
With good liquor I'll make myself mellow —
In an old wicker chair I'll seat myself snug,
Like a jolly and true-hearted fellow.

I'll ne'er trouble my head with the cares of
the nation,
I've enough of my own for to mind,
For the cares of this life are but grief and
vexation,
To death we must all be consigned.

Then I'll laugh, drink, and smoke, and
leave nothing to pay,
But drop like a pear that is mellow,
And when cold in my coffin, I'll leave them
to say,
He's gone! what a true hearted fellow!

AND HOME I CAME MERRY
AT LAST.

Sorrow's a sniviling boy,
Corporal Care's a bore,
I'm for General Joy,
His is a light-hearted corps,
Sing fal de ral, &c.

Gaily my knapsack I slung,
Marching where bullets flew fast!
As loud as they whistled I sung,
And home I came merry at last.
Sing fal de ral, &c.

ROUND.

Love fain did try to sever Friendship's chain,
But as he broke the links, they join'd again;
Friendship with Love united still remain.

538

STEAM BOOTS.

I'll sing you a song, if I possibly can,
Of a Hollander bold, one Mynheer Von Scran,
Whose whole and sole thoughts on invention ran;
In fact he was called a most wonderful man.
    Ri tooral looral, &c.

Now, it chanced that he once was by government sent
On a journey of import, but ere he went,
Says he, ' I shan't ride, for it is my intent,
A pair of new fashioned steam boots to invent.

These boots were made of prodigious size,
For they came full half way up his thighs,
The steamer was fixed, that's right he cries,
For I'm off to-morrow, without gammon or lies.

When morning came, long ere 'twas light,
He was stuck in the street, in the boots upright,
Surrounded by five hundred gazers quite,
Who had all flocked there to see the sight.

Damme I'm off, at length he bawled,
He turned the cock, the women squalled,
Out burst the steam, and the mob appalled,
Was soon in the gutter by dozens sprawled.

Then off like a rocket went poor mynheer,
So swift that his course he could scarcely steer,
Whilst the boots pulled his legs out of joint very near,
And down went all that didn't stand clear.

Near Hamburgh an old turnpike gate stands there,
When bang came the boots with a blow so rare,
They sent it for miles and miles into the air,
And it pitched next morning into Finsbury Square.

Still he travelled away by day and by night,
Dogs, horses, and waggons he sent to flight;
At last he heard with a twinge of affright,
That the soldier wot had the steam arm was in sight.

He soon found out this tale was too true,
For the Arm at a distance appeared in view,
Oh, Lor! cries mynheer, what the deuce shall I do?
For meet him I must and he'll split me in two.

They met! when plump against poor mynheer's face,
Came the noted steam arm, but he still kept his place,
In return gave the soldier a tightish embrace,
Round the neck, while the boots worked on away the
   same pace.

Now the Arm still continued mynheer's face to grind,
Whilst the boots were on each side the soldier entwined
And as they worked on by the steam so inclined,
Why the poor soldier's rump took the blows from
   behind.

Thus they travelled for weeks amid dirt, thumps & pain
Till chancing one day to turn sharp in a lane,
Here they met the Cork Leg, which soon kicked them
   in twain,
Mynheer pitched in Smithfield, the soldier in Spain!

Since this time I suppose you can readily guess,
They've never been seen, no nor heard of much less,
Though they all three got in terrible mess!
L, E, G—A, R, M—B, two O's and T, S. Ri tooral, &c.

BANKS OF Inverary.

Early one summer morning along as I did pass,
On the banks of Inverary I met a bonny lass,
Her hair hung o'er her shoulders broad, her eyes like
   stars did shine,
On the banks of Inverary, I wish she had been mine.

I did embrace this fair maid as long as e'er I could,
Her hair hung o'er he shoulders broad, her eyes like
   drops of dew,
On the banks of Inverary I'm glad to meet with you.

I pray young man give over of embracing of me so,
For after kissing then comes sorrow, after that comes
   woe.
If my poor heart should be ensnared, and I beguil'd
   by thee,
On the banks of Inverary, I am glad you for to see.

Some people say I know you not, but I know you
   said she,
On the banks of Inverary to flatter maids like me;
For once I us'd to flatter maids, but now it must not be,
On the banks of Inverary I found my wife, said he.

I put my horn into my mouth, and blew both loud
   and shrill,
Six of my servant men came out, to wait their master's
   will,
Now will you not consent this night, my charming
   maid said he,
On the banks of Inverary my wedded wife to be.

I'll set my love on horseback, on horseback very high,
We'll go unto some parson without any more delay,
I then will sing all sorts of love, until the day I die;
On the banks of Inverary I first my love did spy.

      [*Spencer, Bradford*]

PLATE No. 37

63

THE
COLLIER SWELL.

I used to be a vulgar clown, with cash and money short in,
Till my old uncle died in town, and left me all his fortune ; .
A collier I was by trade, I have chang'd as you may tell sir,
And since a richer purse I've made, I'd be a regular swell sir.

CHORUS.

But I'm so plagued with vulgar folks,
Since I have cash for sporting,
Why ca'nt a Collier cut a swell,
When he has got a fortune.

I used to go with low-bred chaps, & talk to every gew-gaw,
Get drunk in Tom & Jerry shops and went a purring foot ball ;
But now with all fops in town, I sport my boot and tanners,
And I'm going up to London town to learn some genteel manners.

And when I've been to London town I mean to go to France sir
To practice two or three times a week to learn to hop & dance sir;
Besides I've got a quizzing glass to see things far and near O,
But the other day it caused me to fall over a wheel-barrow.

O my family is a vulgar set, tho' they have clothes in fashion,
They put them on the wrong side out, which puts me in a passion ;
The lads when e'er they go to church, tho' we've got lots of riches,
They all go in their clogs, smock frock and leather breeches.

My wife she is the worst of all when we give genteel dinners,
She uses neither knife nor fork but pops in all her fingers ;
And when they hand the wine about, she tells the gents it stinks
Gets full her mouth, & squirts it out, & calls for treacle drinks.

If I give a dinner to my Lord, and bid her make a good un,
Perhaps she'll make some pea soup, or else a great black pudding ;
And when the tea it is brought in, the tray she always flings sir,
Stirs up the sugar with her fist, & then she licks her fingers.

My lord once ask'd us out to dine & there we had a rum start,
Instead of her new carriage fine, she would ride in the dung cart ;
And when he sent his horse to her, and wanted her to ride sir,
And what do you think of the ignorant jade, she would get on a-
stride sir.

WALKER, PRINTER, DURHAM.

[28]

ANNE LAURIE.

Maxwellton Braes are bonnie,
Where barly fa's the dew ;.
And it's there that Anne Laurie
Gid me her promise true,
Gid me her promise true ;
And ne'er forget will I :
And for bonnie Anne Laurie,
I'll lay down my head and die.

Her skin is like the snow drift,
Her throat is like the swan ;
Her face it is the bonniest
That e'er the sun shone on,
That e'er the sun shone on.
And dark is her blue eye,
And for bonnie Anne Laurie,
I'll lay down my head and die,

Like dew on the gowan lying
Is the fall of her fairy feet,
And like winds in summer sighing,
Her voice is low and sweet,
Her voice is low and sweet.
And she's all the world to me,
And for bonnie Anne Laurie,
I'll lay down my head and die.

PLATE No. 38

We'll Ride the
WAVES TRIUMPHANT

We'll ride the waves triumphant
  With our British Flag unfurl'd,
And tell the mighty Autocrat
  He shall not rule the world;
Tho' his proud ambition tells him
  To be deaf when honour calls,
For well he knows the mighty power
  Of Old England's wooden walls;
Prepare your guns you hearts of oak
  The word will soon be given,
That will send your rattling thunders
      down
  And fall like bolts from heaven,
For a secret spirit's lurking
  Mixed with fire and anxious hope,
To revenge that dreadful slaughter,
  The slaughter of Sinope.
          CHORUS.
Prepare your guns you hearts of oak,
  The word will soon be given,
That will send your rattling thunders
      forth,
  And fall like bolts from heaven;
Our rivers shall keep open,
  And our commerce be at ease,
While brave Dundas and C. Napier
  Shall rule the British seas.

We'll ride the waves triumphant,
  When the Russian fleet is gone
Down to Davy Jones, or claimed
  As England's own;
Then shouts of glorious victory,
  Will be heard from strand to strand
For the spirit of brave Wellington,
  Is hovering o'er the land;
We've gained a mighty ally,
  In Napoleon the Third,
Whose men are made of fire & steel,
  And only wait the word,
For in France still, Moscow's burning
  In the heart of man and child,
So now they go to seek revenge,
  Mid'st cries of vengeance wild.

Beware thou mighty Autocrat,
  Lord Raglan takes the field,
With a French and English army,
  And each man's heart in steel
They with their swords and bayonet,
  Which has prov'd us great renowds
We with our hot artillery
  Will sweep their columns down;
Nay your stronghold at Sabastopol
  Will soon in ruins be,
We will set the proud Hungarians
  And poor suffering Poland free,
Though your number may be millions
  The die of war is cast,
And your noble empire wide and far
  Shall be our own at last.

SLAP-UP
LODGINGS

Bebbington, Printer, 26, Goulden Street Oldham Road
Manchester; sold by J. BEAUMONT, 176,
York Street, Leeds.

When first to town I came, and at the railway landed,
By a fat old dame a card to me was handed,
Says she I'd have you know my name is Mrs. Podgings
I live down this back row, and I let out slap-up lodgings.

We quickly did agree, together we did roam there,
Says she, young man, make free, you'll shortly be at
      home here':
The servant wink'd at me, and so did Mother Podgings
Thinks I I'll have a spree, now I'v got in slap-up lodging

I'd scarce put out the light, when there was such a
      slaughter,   (daughter;
With two chaps who'd a right to court the youngest
The women did murder cry, they knocked down Mother
      Podgings,   (lodgings,
And they broke a lodger's thigh, first night in my new

Just as the clock struck one, and morning was advancing
The each and every one, like madmen fell a-dancing,
But when the chimes went three, they all with Mother
Shout through the key hole to me—   (Podgings.
  (Spoken) Hoy, hoy, old to-ra-laddy, old flummondifuz
how do you like your lodgings.

I then turned round in bed, thinking to have some quiet
When two chaps in the next room said that I made
      the riot;
They pull'd me out of bed, as my name is Peter Hodging
And they shov'd a thing on my head, the use in slap-up
      lodgings.

I little thought, oh dear, they'd got no fellow feeling.
When there came slap-bang in my mouth, a brick from
      the ceiling;
I then down stairs did creep, & said to Mother Podging
I cannot get no sleep, &d—me if I pay for my lodgings

I'd scarce got in the street, out of this here sad house,
For two policemen on their beat, collar'd me for being
      in a bad house,
Six months upon the mill, with ups & downs & dodgings,
I serv'd against my will, thro' being in slap-up lodgings.

PLATE No. 39

The Devil's
IN THE GIRL

It's of a lusty gentlemen, returning from the play,
He knock'd at his true love's door that night with **her to lay**,
She quickly let this young man in and called him her delight,
Saying, roll me in your arms love and lay till morning light.

This fair one was a crafty jade, and unto him did say,
What did please you most love when you was at the play?
He said my dear I've learnt a tune forget it I ne'er shall,
It called a very merry tune 'the devil's in the girl.'

O kind sir let me hear that tune if you your fife can **play**,
I'll listen with attention so now play up I pray,
Oh, the sound it is so beautiful, and pleases me so well,
All night I'll lay if you will play the devil's in the girl.

But the sound awoke her mother all on the second floor,
Who ran down in her bed gown and like a bull did roar,
She spoilt the young man's music she pummeled him **so well**,
Then said the jade he only played the devil's in the girl.

Now this young man quickly left them his journey to pursue,
But mark what followed after this young girl poorly grew,
Her mother said one morning why what's the matter Sal?
You mope about just like a goose the devil's in the girl.

Six months were soon passed over her gown it would'nt **meet**
Her mother finding out the same, she said it was treat,
O daughter said the mother the music's made you swell,
Why it's never good to play the tune, the devil's in the girl.

Twelve months being over this young man out of fun,
He went that way and met the maid who had a lovely son,
She said kind sir come marry me for you can please me well
He shook his head and smiling said, the devil's in the girl.

Oh, if I played the music it pleased you no doubt,
You ought to pay the piper if he the tune played **out**,
So you go your way maid I cannot be your pal,
You may get some other one to play the devil's in **the girl**.

So all you pretty fair maids pray be advised by me,
For you see that I'm rewarded with a baby on my knee,
There is a tune will please you and ruin you as as well,
So, maids beware don't get too near the devil's in the girl.

PLATE NO. 40

COME MARY LINK THI ARM I' MINE

London:—H. P. SUCH, Machine Printer, &
Publisher, 177, Union-street, Boro', S. E.

COME Mary, link thi arm i' mine,
 An' lilt away wi' me,
An' ary that little drop o' brine,
 Froth' corner o' thi c'e ;
Th' mornin' dew i'th heather-bell's
 A bonny gem o' weet,
That tear a different story tells,—
 It pains my heart to see't.
  So Mary, link thi arm i' mine,

No lordly ho' o'th country-side's
 So pleasant to my view,
As th' little cottage where abides
 My bonny lass an' true ;
But ther's a nook beside yon spring,
 Come Mary, share't wi' me,
Aw'll buy tho th' prattiest gowden ring,
 That ever theaw did see.
  So Mary, &c.

My fewther's gan me forty peawnd,
 I' silver an'l gowd,
An' a bonny bit o' garden greawnd,
 O'th morning side o'th fowd ;
An' a handsome bible clean an' new,
 To read for days to come ;
Ther's leyves for writin' names in, too,
 Like th' owd un at's awhoam.
  So Mary, &c.

Eawr Jenny's bin buyin' in,
 An' every day hoo brings
Knives an' forks an' pots an' irons,
 For smoothin' caps an' things :

My granny's sent a chest o' drawes,
 Sunday clooas to keep in ;
'An' little Fanny's bought a glass
 For thee an' me to peep in.
  So Mary, &c.

Eawr Tum as sent a bacon-flitch,
 Eawr Jem a load o' coals,
Eawr Charlie's bought some pictures, an'
 He's hanged em upoth' woles ;
Owd Posys white-weshod th' cottage
  through,
 Eawr Matty's made it sweet,
An' Jack's gan me his Jarman flute,
 To play by the fire at neet.
  So Mary, &c.

There's cups an' saucers an' porritch pons,
 An' tables, geyt an' smo ;
There's brushes, mugs an' ladens cans,
 An' Eight-day clock an' o'
There's a cheer for thee an' one for me,
 An' one i' every nook,
Thi mother's as a cushion on it,
 It's th' nicest cheer i'th took,
  So Mary, &c.

My mother's gan me th' four-post bed,
 Wi' curtains to't an' o'
An' pillows, sheets an' bowster too,
 As white as driven snow ;
It isn't stuffed wi' fither deawn,
 But th' flocks are clean an' new,
Hoo says ther's honest folks i'th teawn,
 That made a warse, an' do.
  So Mary, &c.

Aw peeped into my cot last neet,
 It made me hutchin' fain,
A bonny fire wur winkin bright,
 I' every window pane.
Aw marlock'd upo'th white hearthstone,
 An' dreamed o'th kittle lid,
An' sung " My neest is snug an' sweet,
 Aw 'il go and fetch my bride."
  So Mary, &c.

 617.

Written Music for the **Violin, Flute, Accordian, Cornopeon**
Instruction Books for all kinds of Instruments.

You don't know what you can do till you try.

Toys. Violins Accordians & Concertinas sold & repaired.

I've been a gav youth in my time,
But thanks to my parents for that,
Whom they were I cannot define.
It's a doubtful affair, and that's flat.
I was won at a raffle, no doubt,
So am nobody's child, by the bye—
So I said to myself, look about—
You don't know what you can do till you try.

Grim poverty's clutches ne'er dread,
Be resolute—never say die—
Keep continually going a-head—
You don't know what you can do till you try.

A ragged young scamp 'bout the street,
I was—till one day in her arms,
A lady took me, dressed me neat,
And greatly admiring my charms,
Said, she'd be my mamma, if I'd quick,
Go with her and live upon pie—
Oh, won't I, says I, like a brick,
You don't know what you can do till you try.

So she took home her ready-made child,
And made me a smart looking lad,
So by me " dear mamma" she was styled,
For she was the first I had had.
Of a morning 'fore she was awake,
When six-pennoth of ha'pence high,
Her hard cash I swooped for hardbake—
You don't know what you can do till you try.

One day I caught hold of a gun,
And off to the garden I went,
Determined on having some fun,
If it was but a pop at a cat.
Tried to hit a game cock in the head,
That stood on a green-house elose by,
Shot my newly found mother instead,
You don't know what you can do if you try.

The loss of my parent I grieved,
Till I found she had left me some cash.
So as soon as the tin I received,
I beleive I came out abit splash !
With the girls I had many a freak,
For I'd grown big enough, by the bye—
Spent four hundred pounds in a week—
You don't know what you can do, if you try.
Grim poverty's &c

I lost nothing by cutting a shine,
For one evening I was at a ball—
Introduced to an heiress divine,
Was accepted—my face did it all.
We were married instanta, egad,
I sowed my wild oats instantly,
And reaped a nice fortune, my lad,
You don't know what you can do if you try
Grim poverty's, &c.

We'd married been, nearly three years,
And no pledges of love had appear'd,
My spousey was nearly in tears—
We're to have none, says she I'm afeeard.
Friends joked us in innocent mirth,
Don't be in a hurry, says I—
The next year she'd three at a birth—
You don't know what you can do if you try.
Grim poverty's, &c.

Of sorrows—(now mark what I say)—
No matter how deeply you sup,
The pleasures you'll taste of some day,
Let your motto be " never give up !"
Through working the oracle well,
From the lowlands I've jumped to the high,
So may you— persevere—who can tell ?
You don't know what you can do till you try.
Grim poverty's, &c.

Instruments bought, sold or exchanged. Fancy Walking sticks

Printed by T. King, Birmigham, and sold by Mr. Green, at his Music Stall, near the Turnpike, City-road, and at 27, Featherstone-street City-road, where an extensive collection of old and new songs, harp and violin strings, fancy stationery, &c., may be had.

Tamborines, bows, screws, bridges, rosin, music paper,

Plate No. 42

MY WIFE'S FIRST BABY

The other night I lay in my bed
   Along with my wife Mrs. Bunning,
She said, Tom, for the doctor pray run,
   For I think our first baby is coming ;
I dressed myself quick you'll suppose,
   The snow on the ground was fast falling,
Shut the door and was cutting away,
   When the policeman sent me sprawling.

Hollo ! my fine fellow, said he,   [bour,
   You've been robbing the house of a neigh-
In vain I implored to be free,
   And I told him my wife was in labour;
Said he then you'll soon follow suit,
   For confined you'll be I'll maintain,
To the station with me you must go,
   Your tale is all labour in vain.

The inspector on duty I knew,   [ner,
   And got off well pleased with his man-
For he said the policeman should go
   And find out the nurse Mrs. Tanner;
To the wrong house he went, and then
   Very loud at the door began knocking,
O ! they emptied the contents of the po
   On his head, & he looked very shocking.

The doctor he made matters right,   [baby,
   And brought forth the precious young
Which good reason I've got to deplore,
   For the treatment I got is so shabby;

My bed is like one in a garden,
   Well watered each night, and I'm sure
You will pity my case when I say,
   On my legs I oft find some manure.

Sometimes I'm awoke in the night
   By the child kicking up a great rout,
Out of bed I'm obliged for to get,
   And I trot the young fellow about;
But the weather is so very cold,
   To pity me you'll be inclin'd,
For my shirt that is wet through & through
   Keeps flapping against me behind.

The folks tell me not to mind,
   My feelings I always should smother.
Tho' this may be all very well,   [ther
   But my wife she will soon have ano
She is such a rum un to go,
   I ought to have plenty of riches.
In the family way she will fall,
   If I on the bed throw my breeches.

Of this to my wife I complain,   [strik
   And I tell her the game she shoul
But she says it's my fault and not her's,
   She'll have the whole lot 'cause she likes
So I try to bear up all I can,   [it;
   Tho' I own I'm a bit of a grum bier.
Yet it's best for to give it them well, [bler
   Than to be called by the women a fum

34

FIFTEEN SHILLINGS A WEEK.

MARY MACHREE

THE flower of the valley was Mary Machree,
Her smiles all bewitching were lovely to see,
The bees round her humming when summer was
    gone,
And the roses were fled, might take her lip for one
Her laugh it was music, her breath it was balm,
Her heart, like the lake, was as pure and as calm,
Till love o'ercame, like a breeze o'er the sea,
And made the heart heave of sweet Mary Machree.

She loved and she wept, nor was sadness e'er known
To dwell in the bosom that love makes its own ;
His joys are but moments, his griefs are for years,
He comes all in smiles, but he leaves all in tears.
Her lover was gone to a far distant land,
And Mary in sickness would pace the lone strand,
And tearfully gaze on the dark rolling sea,
That parted her lover from Mary Machree.

FIFTEEN SHILLINGS A

A MAN and his wife in —— street,
with seven children young and sweet,
Had a jolly row last night comple e,
    About fifteen shillings a week, sir.
He gave his wife a clumsy clout,
Saying how is all my money laid out,
Tell me quickly, he did shout,
And then she soon did set about,
Reckoning up without delay,
what she laid out from day to day,
You shall know what's done, the wife did say,
    with fifteen shillings a week, sir.

Seven children to feed and find in clothes,
And to his wife he did propose,
To reckon how the money goes,
His fifteen shillings a week, sir.

Threepence halfpe ny, a week for milk is spent,
One and ninepence a week for rent,
For the child a penny for pepp rmint,
    Out of fifteen shilling a week, sir.
For tobacco eightp nce e e y week,
Half a crown for but her's m at,
And to make your tea compl t,
A three farthing bloater for a treat,

A penny a week for cotton and thread,
Last Sunday tenpence a small sheep's head ;
Ninepence halfpenny a day for bread,
    Out of fifteen shillings a week, sir.

Potatoes for dinner there must be found,
And there's none for less than a penny a pound,
I often have a sixpenny gown,
    Out of fifteen shillings a week, sir.
A haporth of starch and a farthing blue,
Twopence halfpenny soap and potash too,
A pennorth of onions to make a stew,
Three halfpence a day small beer for you.
Instead of butter, sixpennorth of fat,
And to wipe your shoes a twopenny mat,
with a halfpenny a day to feed the cat,
    Out of fifteen shillings a week, sir.

Ninepence a week for old dry peas,
Sixpence sugar and eighteence tea;
Pepper, salt, and mustard, farthings three,
    Out of fifteen shillings a week, sir.
One and tenpence halfpenny understand,
Every week for firing out of hand,
Threepence halfpenny candles a farthing sand,
And threepence to bottom the frying pan ;
A twopenny broom to sweep the dirt,
Three haporth of cloth to mend your shirt,
Now don't you think you are greatly hurt
    Out of fifteen shillings a week, sir ?

Clothes for Tommy, Dick, Sal, Polly, and Jane,
And Jimmy and Betty must have the same ;
You had a sixpenny jacket in Petticoat lane
    Out of fifteen shillings a week, sir ;
For shaving a halfpenny twice a week,
A penny to cut your hair so neat.
Threepence for the socks upon your feet,
Last week you bought a tenpenny seat,
Besides, old chap, I had most forgot,
You gave a penny for a kidney pie all hot,
And threepence for an old brown chamber pot,
    Out of fifteen shillings a week, sir.

So now old chap you plainly see,
If you can reckon as well as me,
There is little waste in our family,
    Out of fifteen shillings a week, sir.
There's many a woman would think no sin
To spend the whole in snuff and gin ;
When again to reckon you do begin,
Recollect there's a farthing a week for pins;
To make things right my best I've tried,
That's economy, can't be denied.
Dear wife said he, I'm satisfied,
    Out of fifteen shillings a week.

So you women all the kingdom through,
To you this might appear quite new,
Just see if you the same can do,
    with fifteen shillings a week, oh.

THE
PAWNBROKER'S
SHOP.

JOHN HARKNESS, PRINTER, 121, CHURCH STREET, PRESTON.

A song I will recite to you,
I hope it will delight you,
I am sure it will not fright you.
It is the place to rise the cash,
Where you may cut a mighty dash ;
It is kept by Mr. Flute,
Indeed what I say is truth,
I dare say that he has seen you,
It is kept by Mr. Ball,
Where the La lies often call,
For to leave a tippet or shawl.
At the sign of two to one,
At the sign of the Golden Ball.

(Spoken)—Now my little girl what have you got in
your hand ? A flat iron, sir, my mother wants six-
pence on it. I suppose your mother thinks we are
all flats ; we never lend more than fourpence on a flat
iron. My mother says you would much oblige her
if you would lend her sixpence on it, as she is going
to have company, and she wants some butter and
some sugar, and some of the best tea- Will four-
pence do ? Why I suppose it must if you won't lend
more. Here, Jack, make a ticket for a flat iron, four-
pence.—My turn next. What for you ? Ninepence
on this old shirt. What have you made of the tail of
it ? I will ask my husband when I go home. Now,
my man, what for you ? Twenty-pence on this old
coffee pot. Why it smells very rummy. No, sir,
my mother keeps gin in it. What is your mother's
name—Jackey ?

What crowding and what squeezing,
You would hardly get your knees in,
It is so very teazing,
I'm wedged, I can't get out,
O hang the cursed spout.
I should not care a button,
If I only got some mutton,
For my father's such a glutton,
And he thinks it's nearly done.

(Spoken)—Now Mr. Ball, I want my husband's
breeches and stockings. There is some one before you.
What for you Mr. Dandy ? I want you to oblige me
with the loan of ten guineas on my violin. Ten fid-
dle-sticks you mean, I suppose, I cannot lend more
than twenty-five shillings on a violin. But, sir, it is
real crimona, I pledge my honnour. No I'll be hang'd

if you do, you may pledge your fiddle, but honour we
don't take in here. Now my good woman, what in
the name of God have you got there ? My husband's
wooden leg. Then you are determined your husband
shall not give you leg bail. What his your husband's
name ? Pop-and-go. Here John make a ticket for Pop-
and-go's wooden leg, two-and-sixpence—I want my
husband's Sunday coat, for he is going to chapel to-
morrow, and I must have it out, and I want to leave
you this riding habit in exchange. Well good woman,
I am glad to see some signs of reformation in you.
What do you mean by that ? I think it is a sign you
are going to get rid of some of your old habits. I'll
let you know they are almost new. Now Mr. Ball,
don't stand there making such a noise, but serve us
and let us go. What do you want ? I want a beaver
hat and box, in the name of Felt,

Now Saturday night's the time, sir,
Of fun to see the prime, sir,
Just about half-past nine, sir,
That is the time to spout.
Give me my shirt, I pray,
For I want to go away,
In the week I have but one day,
To-morrow, that is Sunday ;
I'll bring it again on Monday,
If you'll only let me out.

(Spoken)—Now Tickets—now Mrs. Jones, how
many for you ? Twenty-five. They are all here but
a flat iron and looking glass. I must have the flat
iron to-night, for I want to iron my husband's shirt,
and the glass he will miss very soon in the morning.
Now, Mrs. Dashall, I am very sorry I cannot tell
where your ear-rings are. But I must have them to-
night, sir, for I am going to a party to-morrow, and
must have them out. Now Mr. Carpenter, what for
you ? I want my saw, for I have got a job to go to
to-morrow, and I must have it out. John, did you
see any thing of this gentleman's saw. No sir, saw
nothing but a chisel. D—n it, do you think I am
going to be chisled out of my saw in that manner.
You must not make such a noise in my shop, there
is some before ; Felt, what do you want ? A beaver
hat and box : I have been waiting all night. Well,
here is the beaver hat and box, six shillings and
three-half-pence farthing. Well, here is six and
three-half-pence, and you owed me a farthing last
time. Success to Mr. Balls.

229

PLATE No. 45

ESMERALDA.

T. Pearson, Printer,
4 & 6, Chadderton St., Oldham Road,
Manchester.

Written by Andrew Halliday, Esq.
Composed by W. C. Levey.
Music to be had at Messrs Duff & Stewart,
147, Oxford Street, London, W.

Sung by
Madame Rudersdorff, Mdlle. Liebhart,
Madame Bodda Pyne, and Miss Furtado,
In the "Adelphi" Drama of "Notre Dame."

Also Sung by Miss Kate Bella, in all
the Leading London & Provincial Music Halls.

WHERE is the little Gipsy's home?
Under the spreading greenwood tree,
Wherever she may roam.
Where'er that tree may be;
Roaming the wide world o'er,
Crossing the deep blue sea.
She finds on ev'ry shore,
A home among the free,
She finds on ev'ry shore,
A home among the free.
   Ah, Voilà, La Gitana, Voilà, La Gitana,
  Esmeralda, Esmeralda, Zingara,
      Voilà, La Gitana, &c.

The Gipsy is like the bird,
A bird, that sings in tree and bow'r,
The Gipsy is like the Bee,
The Bee, that flits from flow'r to flow'r;
She loves the sun and sky,
She loves the song and dance,
The groves of sunny Spain,
The plains of La Belle France, La Belle France.
   Ah, Voilà La Gitana, Voilà La Gitana,
    Voilà La Gitana, &c.
Oh, leave her like the bird to sing,
To sing on ev'ry tree and bow'r,
Oh, leave her like the Bee,
To flit from flow'r to flow'r;
Roaming the wide world o'er,
Crossing the deep blue sea
She finds on ev'ry shore,
A home among the free,
She finds on ev'ry shore.
A home among the free.
   Ah, Voilà, La Gitana, Voilà, La Gitana,
  Esmeralda, Esmeralda, Esmeralda, Zingara,
      Voilà, La Gitana, &c.

No. 763.

DO EVERYONE AS YOU CAN!

JOHN HENRY SHARP, is my name,
  Henry Slow it was once,
But experience, dull men make wise,
  And educates the dunce:
In my career I've been done,
  And cheated here and there,
Been welched at Races, sharped at cards,
  And thought each friend was fair.
      Chorus:
  Do everybody as clean as you can,
    Is a griffin, I give that's true,
  And take particular notice, that—
    Nobody ever does you.

I've studied Horse and Billards,
  Racing, Cards and Loo,
And as I have often been done before,
  What now I mean to do;
To do, is this, that I wont be done,
  If I am, why, I'm to blame.
Tho' they have had me, now, I'll have them,
  Flat-caching is my game.

When first I tried to sing a song,
  Or, tried myself to engage,
I found the road was very hard,
  To prosper on the stage;
I've had applause, and ten pounds a week,
  That don't suit now, you see,
For I've doubled it twice or thrice,
  Or, the Managers dont have me.

When you get married, have a fair start,
  For crosses are many in life,
And don't be cross, with the girl you love,
  Or, Master, will be the wife;
Now, don't be cross, and don't be cruel,
  Steer clear thro' married life,
And whatever you do, do on the sly,
  Then you neatly do the wife.

FATHER, DEAR FATHER,

FATHER, dear father, come home with me now,
  The clock in the steeple strikes *one*;
You said you were coming right home from the shop,
  As soon as your day's work was done;
Our fire has gone out, our house is all dark,
  And mother's been watching since tea,
With poor little Benny so sick in her arms,
  And no one to help her but me.
Come home, come home, come home,
Please Father, dear father, come home.

Father, dear father, come home with me now,
  The clock in the steeple strikes *two*;
The night has grown colder, and Benny is worse,
  And he has been calling for you;
Indeed he is worse ma says he will die,
  Perhaps before morning shall dawn;
And this is the message she sent me to bring,
  Come quickly, or he will be gone.
Come home, come home, come home,
Please father, dear father, come home.

Father, dear father, come home with me now,
  The clock in the steeple strikes *three*;
The house is so lonely, the hours are so long,
  For poor weeping mother and me;
Yes, we are alone, poor Benny is dead,
  And gone with the angels of light;
And these were the very last words that he said,
  I want to kiss father,—to-night.
Come home, come home, come home,
Please father, dear father, come home.

REPLY OF THE FATHER.

GO home to thy mother, go home, leave me now,
  I care not if the clock has struck one,
Go home to thy mother, I'll not come I vow
  Till this game of cards I have done.
Go tell her that candles and coals she must buy,
  I gave her a sixpence at morn;
I care not though your brother Benny should die,
  I happy shall be when he's gone,
Go home, go home, go home,
Tell mother that father won't come.

Go home to thy mother, go home, leave me now,
  I care not if the clock has struck two;
I feel not the cold, though your brother is worse,
  He calls not for me, but for you.
Your pleadings are vain, I'll come when I like,
  Its useless to plead, that I'll prove,
Go tell her this message, don't tempt me to strike,
  I shall not from this house remove.
Go home, go home, go home,
Tell mother that father won't come.

Go home to thy mother, stay, what have I said?
  You tell me the clock has struck three,
O God, can it be that my poor boy is dead,
  And mourned for by mother and thee.
Yes, yes, my child, with thee I'll go,
  In future more steady will live,
And you pray to God, and poor Benny above,
  Your father's past sins to forgive.
I'll come, I'll come, I'll come,
My dear child, thy father will come.

NO HOME LIKE THE DRUNKARD'S.

Tune—Home, Sweet Home.

NO home like the drunkard's for sorrow and care
  No wife so distressed, no children so bare;
With pale sunken features, they cry still in vain,
Ye friends of humanity, break the fell chain.

Strong drink like a demon has smitten our isle,
Its pestilent poison is still to defile.
It brought us to madness, and sorrow and pain,
Arise in your manhood and break the fell chain.

How happy the nation, the home and the heart,
When free from the sins which strong drink doth impart,
When husbands and wives and their children agree,
How pleasant! how happy! how holy and free.

Arise, then, ye heralds of mercy, arise,
The life of a coward for ever despise;
March onward, the strongholds of Bacchus assail,
And trust in the Lord, and the truth will prevail.

THE BRADFORD CHIMNEY DISASTER.

THE morning bursts forth in gladness,
  The wind is sharp and chill;
Ne'er dreaming of evening's sadness,
  They hie towards the mill.

They hear the noisy engine start,
  And to their posts they go;
The wheels now hum, the shuttles dart
  And whistle to and fro.

The morning flies, 'tis breakfast time,
  The time for lunch and spree;
Alas! ye in that dreadful room,
  Shall there no warning be?

Oh, Fate! hold back thine horrid hand,
  See, the souls in yonder;
But, Ah! he waves his dreadful wand,
  Now a crash like thunder.

Walls fall in, timbers creak and rend,
  Loud shrieks now fill the air;
Huge beams and stones rear on an end,
  Now cries of dread despair.

The dreadful crash, and dust and steam,
  Bring crowds of people round
To know what means so strange a scene,
  And all that deaf'ning sound.

The fiery fiend now tells his tale,
  There, 'neath the debris lay
Calm, motionless, and deadly pale,
  Some forms of mangled clay.

The sobs of parents now we hear,
  One shrieks in accents wild,
See, on that horrid stretcher there,
  Some men bring out her child.

The youthful forms thus snatched away,
  Cause hearts to burn with woe;
And think and act in blank dismay
  While tears unceasing flow.

Next we behold long funeral trains,
  And then the broken sod,
'Neath which we laid their last remains,
  Their souls are left with God.

JOSEPH ELLIS, Printer, Heckmondwike & Liversedge.

PLATE No. 47

NEWCASTLE

Town Moor Amusements

AT WHITSUNTIDE:

Or, The Pitman's Journey from Benwell,

TO SEE SIMPSON THE PEDESTRIAN.

A NEW SONG.

Tune—"*Derry Down &c.*"

TWAS on Whiffen Monday wor Peg and wor Tom,
  Wor Geordy and Jenny, to Newcastle all com,
Left Benwell High Cross, wor canny bit hyem,
To fee the great Walker, yen Simfon by nyem.
Derry down, &c.

'Twas about yen o'clock when we gave ower wark,
Aw wefh'd myfel clean, and put on a wheyre fark.
Be fharp! fays wor Jenny, or we'll lof a' the fun;
Wey hinny! fays aw, the gam's nobb't begun.
Derry down, &c.

To the Race Ground we gat, 'twas juft half paft three,
An' glowr'd a' about, the Pedeftrian to fee;
At laft he comes fweating, and walking fe faft,
It was juft like a feyer-flaught as he went paft.
Derry down, &c.

He's a great lang auld fellow, upon fhankey's naig,
About fix feet twee or three inches, 'tis faid;
His age fixty-fix—but aw think that's a hum,
He juft tells the folks that to get them to come.
Derry down, &c.

'Tis nine miles an hour they fay, at wor town,
He's to walk without ftopping until he be's done,
And that's not till Tuefday, late or i' the day,
So if he's not duin, fmash my fark! he weel may.
Derry down, &c.

Oh Geordy, fays Peggy what feuls we've a' been!
Aw thowt to fee wonders and wonders aw've feen,
A man walking as we fee—is that all that's here?
Come, howay to Benwell, there's far mair fport there.
Derry down &c.

Ye may talk of the fun and the fpree ye hev here,
The fine ftreets and churches and a' yor good beer;
But wor Hoppin at Benwell's far better than a'
The grand feets at Newcaffel that ever aw faw.
Derry down, &c.

How Wilfon will fret fhould this chep win the day,
For he's wager'd a bottle he cannot, they fay;
He thowt there was nyen that could beat him in walking,
But fhould this fellow win it will fpoil all his talking.
Derry down, &c.

Marfhall, Printer, Newcaftle.

PLATE No. 48

LONG-SONG SELLER.

"Two under fifty for a fardy'?"

NEVER MAIDS WED
AN
Old Man.

Sec. 3

This old man he courted me, hey down derry down,
This old man he courted me, hey derry down
This old man he courted me, his bride for to be,
Never maids while you live wed an old man.

O when we did go to church, hey down derry down
O when we did go to church, hey derry down,
O when we did go to church his money he did begrudge
Never maids while you live wed an old man.

O when we sat down to meat, hey down derry down,
O when we sat down to meat, hey derry down,
O when we sat down to meat, he never bade me eat,
Never maids while you live wed an old man.

O when we did go to bed, hey down derry down,
O when we did go to bed, hey derry down,
O when we did go to bed, he lay as if he were dead,
Never maids while you live wed an old man.

I laid my hand on his breast, hey down derry down,
I laid my hand on his breast hey derry down,
I laid my hand on his breast, he swore he could get no
            rest,
Never maids while you live wed an old man.

I laid my leg over him, hey down derry down,
I laid my leg over him, hey derry down,
I laid my leg over, he swore I would smother him,
Never maids while you live wed an old man.

So when he fell fast asleep, hey down derry down,
So when he fell fast asleep, hey derry down,
So when he fell fast asleep, out of bed I did creep,
Into the arms of a jolly young man.

And there we did sport and play, hey down derry down,
And there we did sport and play, hey derry down,
And there we did sport and play, until the break of day,
Never maids while you live wed an old man.

THE
GUILD
—o—

Dear cousin you know I promis'd to write,
I am safely arriv'd, though I travelled all night.,
I'll sing you a song if you'll not take it ill,
And I'll tell you the fun I had at Preston Guild.
    There were tailors and tanners of leather,
    Weavers and Coopers together,
    And there we had such charming weather.
On the day I arrived at the Guild.

To see the great sight I soon got a good place,
It surprised the world with beauty and grace;
There were feathers and flowers and bosoms like snow,
In beautiful ringlets their hair did flow.
    The ladies procession was walking,
    The noblemen laughing and talking,
    While each jolly farmer stood gaping,
    To catch all the fun at the Guild.

Trades of all kinds were busy at work,
Making goods that were useful for Christian or Turk
To get at the goods there was a great rout,
For as fast as they made them they threw them about
    There were constables doing their duty,
    And ladies exposing their beauty,
    And pick-pockets making their booty,
    The time that I staid at the Guild.

Such thrutching, and sqeezing, and squalling between
Such tearing of clothes sure never was seen,
Such rattling of coaches—upsetting of gigs,
With the loss of their garters, their aprons and wigs.
    There were some with their petticoats trailing,
    And some their new bonnets bewailing,
    With the boys tumbling over the railing,
    To get a full view of the Guild.

There was mutton and beef, baked roasted and boil'd,
With cordials for women and cakes for the child,
There were sausages, puddings, and ginger-bread hot
With potatoes and dumplings hot out of the pot.
    There were hungry cildren crying,
    While some with their thirst were a dying.
    And others fat bacon were frying,
    On the day I arrived at the Guild.

So now to conclude and finish my song,
My good people, I hope I've not kept you too long,
May heaven preserve you, and keep you from ill,
And spare you to go to the next Preston Guild.
    For a credit it is to the nation,
    Success to each trade in its station,
    And God save the Queen and the Nation,
    That maintains the just right of the Guild.

PLATE No. 49

Newcastle & London BOAT MATCH,

FOR £100 ASIDE.

ON SATURDAY, JULY 16. TUNE-'THE CAMPBELL'S ARE COMIN'.'

Let canny Newcastle once more raise her
   head,   [tho' she were dead;
From the sod where she's long moan'd as
Let the sons of the Tyne once again bear
   the sway,   (race to day.
And though poverty reigns, gain the boat
For the pride of our navy, Northumber-
   land's sons   [ed our guns,
Have long mann'd our yards and direct-
May the Keel row and Boatie-row still
   grace the river,   (ever.
And canny Newcastle yet flourish for

For ages long past have our seamen been
   famed,   (are named;
And Newcastle's blue jackets aye foremost
On the topmast of fame long has Colling-
   wood stood,   (the flood
The dread of our foes and the pride of
Then to day let the skill of the past be
   display'd,   [afraid,
Nor of England's first boat crew be ever
Invincible long, may St. Agnes' crew
   reign,   [main !
The boast of Newcastle, the pride of the
    For the pride of our navy, &c

Combes, Newell, and Parish, the pride of
   the Thames,   (names;
Have in many boat races exalted their
But the pride of the Tyne they contend
   with to day,   [them the way
And Newcastle's bright flag may direct
May the oars of the Glaspers be pull'd
   well together,   [to the weather,
May their strength never fail as they bend

May the Agnes fly over the waves like a
   swallow.   (pletely beat hollow.
And the Cockneys brave crew be com-

    For the pride of our navy, &c.

How proud seems each head as it bends
   o'er the waves.   (er than slaves;
Though our pitmen and seamen work hard
How bright is each eye, and how light is
   each heart,   [for the start.
As the boats are preparing and manned
The signal is given, they glide o'er the
   stream.   (ning's gleam ;
Like the arrow's swift glance, or the light-
Tho' we wish them all well, may the Ag-
   nes display,   (to day.
For the pride of Newcastle, a conquest

    For the pride of Newcastle, &c

May our canny blue jackets, our pitmen
   and lasses,   [glasses ;
Dance lightly to night and replenish their
May misfortune's foul wind leave New-
   castle to day,
And prosperity's sun shed a happier ray.
May friendship and harmony reign in
   each heart,   [don they start,
And the Cockneys confess when for Lon-
That the sons of Newcastle, tho' homely
   and plain,   [the main.
Are the pride of the lasses, the stars of

    For the pride of Newcastle, &c

No. 25.

T. DODDS, PRINTER, HEAD OF THE SIDE *1842*

PLATE No. 50

THE INDIAN MAID.

OH this was the cot of the Indian Maid,
And the bow'r where youth fond tribute paid,
She'd ev'ry charm but a heart they say,
For that young Selim she'd given away,
No heart could heighten, or beauty could aid
The roseate smiles of the Indian Maid.

But Selim was false to the Indian Maid,
No longer the youth fond tribute paid.
The heart she had given he broke they say,
And in wild despair she travers'd the day,
No words can heighten the sorrow that prey'd,
On the wounded heart of the Indian Maid.

Steer My Bark.

Oh, I have roamed o'er many lands,
And many friends I've met,
Not one fair scene or kindly smile,
Can this fond heart forget;
But I'll confess that I'm content,
No more I'd wish to roam,
O steer my bark to Erin's isle,
For Erin is my home.

In Erin's isle there's manly hearts,
And bosoms pure as snow,
In Erin's isle there's right good cheer,
And hearts that ever flow,
In Erin's isle I'd pass my time,
No more I'd wish to roam,
O steer my bark to Erin's isle,
For Erin is my home.

If England was my place of birth,
I'd love her tranquil shore,
If bonnie Scotland was my home,
Her mountains I'd adore;
But pleasant days in both I've past,
I'll dream of days to come,
O steer my bark to Erin's isle,
For Erin is my home.

HE'S GOT NO COURAGE IN HIM.

As I walked out one Summer's morning,
    To view the trees and leaves a springing,
I saw two Birds upon a tree,
    Chirping thir notes and sweetly singing
                O dear O.

I saw two Maidens standing by,
    One of them her hands was wringing,
And all her conversation was,
    My husband's got no courage in him.
                O dear O,

All sorts of meat I do provide,
    All sorts of drink that is fit for him,
Both Oysters, pies, and Rhubarb too,
    But nothing can put courage in him.
                O dear O.

My husband can caper, dance, or sing,
    And do any thing that is fit for him,
But he cannot do the thing I want,
    For alas he's got no courage in him.
                O dear O.

Seven long years I made his bed,
    Six of them I've lain beside him,
This morning I arose with an aching head,
    That shows he's got no courage in him.
                O dear O,

If he does not shortly try,
    A cuckold I am sure to make him,
For let me do whatever I will,
    I cannot put courage in him.
                O dear O.

Come all fair maid wherever you be,
    Don't have a man before you try him,
Don't have to sing a song like me,
    My husband's got no courage in him.
                O dear O

No. 41.

A copy of verses on the sorrowful lamentation of

Thomas Stew

Who now lies under the Awful sentence of Death, in Kirkdale Gaol for the Wilful Murder of his Sweetheart, Alice Nolan, whom he Murdered July the 7th, 1844.

Harkness, Printer, 121, Church Street, Preston.

Ye young men and maidens wherever you be,
I pray give attention and listen to me :
I loved Alice Nolan as dear as my life,
And many times wished that she'd be my wife.

I loved young Alice sincerely and true,
And sometimes I thought she loved me too,
Being anxious to gain her, to church then I went
And put up the askings without her consent.

Told what I'd done, when she to me did say,
Tom Stew thou will never see my wedding day
Twas a fatal moment, cursed jealously then,
Like a flash of lightning did enter my brain.

On the 7th of July, oh curs'd be that day,
At a friend's house in Cook Street, we both did
take tea,
She seemed so cheerful, so merrily joked,
I thought her mind chang'd her denial revok'd.

I ask'd her again but she answered not yet,
And no other promise from her I could get,
I rose up in anger, with jealously burn'd,
I borrowed a razor then to her return'd.

I asked her out we together did walk,
Till we got to Shaw Brow, about love we did talk
I said dearest Alice you shall be my bride,
Then shall we be married, not yet she replied.

You do love some other unto her I said,
Then deep cross her throat I drew the razor-
blade :
Oh God she exclaimed then staggered aside,
To the door of a neighbour and instantly died.

Her innocent blood flow'd in streams to the
ground,
The neighbours alarmed did soon gather round,
Assistance was vain for poor Alice was dead,
And unto its maker her spirit had fled

I was seized with remorse as I ran down the
hill,
Then resolved that instant myself for to kill,
Then with the same razor close by Shepherd's
door,
I cut my own throat then sunk down on the floor

Unto the infirmary I was conveyed,
Where they healed the wound I so rasely had
made ;
At Liverpool assizes my trial came on,
I was cast and condemned for the deed I had done

I swooned away when condemned to die,
While the court it was filled with an heartrend-
ing cry
From my poor old mother, who stood there to see
And hear her son sentenced to die on a tree.

In the condemned cell the sad hour I await,
When for murdering my true love I must meet
my fate,
God help her poor mother and likewise my own,
They will suffer sorely when I'm dead and gone

So young men and maidens who hear my sad tale
Resist when curst jealousy does you assail,
Thro' jealousey love of to hatred will turn,
It has prov'd my downfall & curs'd me to mourn

356.

PLATE No. 52

THE CRUEL
Sea Captain
AND
NANCY OF YARMOUTH.

John Harkness, Printer, Church-Street, Preston.

It is of a sea Captain in Yarmouth did dwell,
He courted young Nancy, a comely young girl,
Because she was handsome with her rolling black eyes,
Pretty Nancy of Yarmouth all the world could surprise.

One day she was walking in a shady green grove,
So melodiously singing her sweet songs of love,
Her voice charmed the small birds, young Edward was near,
Then to Nancy of Yarmouth young Edward did steer.

Good morning, my fair one, young Edward did say,
I have just received orders for London straightway,
Be constant to your Edward who is constant you know,
So he lured pretty Nancy with young Edward to go.

They started for London—pretty Nancy did cry,
Saying farewell sweet home, then tears rolled from each eye,
Pray be true to your Nancy— I'll be constant, said he,
If we safe reach famed London then united we'll be.

They arrived in London to his friends the next day,
Those words pretty Nancy was heard for to say,
I have jewels to entice me, and diamonds so fine,
But the honour of Nancy more brilliant shall shine.

Three months had pass'd over when Edward did say,
I am called to the ocean, I will boldly obey,
So yield to my embraces you shall ne'er be my wife,
Or Nancy of Yarmouth I will end your life.

A cup of strong poison on the table did stand,
And a bright barrell'd pistol he held in each hand,
Now yield or drink poison, he loudly did cry,
Pretty Nancy of Yarmouth then consented to die.

That instant pretty Nancy she turn'd with a frown,
She seized both the pistols, and knock'd Edward down,
Lay there, cruel creature—pretty Nancy she said,
You may take your strong poison, still Nancy's a maid.

She pack'd up her clothing, to her friends she did go,
And told them that Edward had used her so,
Then she gain'd their forgiveness—was beloved as before
So it's best to be virtuous, if you're ever so poor.

Farewell
TO YOUR
JUDGES
AND
JURIES.

—→→●●●←←—

Here's adieu to your judges and juries,
    Justices and Old Baileys also,
Seven years he's transported my true-love,
    Seven years he's transported you know.

To go to a strange country don't grieve me,
    Nor leaving Old England behind,
It's all for the sake of my Polly, love,
    And leaving my parents behind,

There's the Captain that is our Commander,
    The Boatswain and the ship's crew,
There is married men too, and there's single,
    Who knows what we transports do.

Dear Polly I'm going to leave you,
    For seven long years, love, and more,
But that time will be but a moment,
    When return'd to the girl I adore.

If ever I return from the ocean,
    Stores of riches I'll bring for my dear,
It's all for the sake of my Polly love,
    I'll cross the salt seas for my dear.

How hard is the place of confinement,
    That keeps me from my hearts delight,
Cold chains and irons surround me,
    And a plank for my pillow at night.

How often I wish that the eagle,
    Would lend me her wing I would fly,
Then I'd fly to the arms of my Polly, love,
    And on her soft bosom I'd live.

[The following Song, by G. P. CODDEN, (very popular in the North of England,) was printed and presented to the Auditory, at a Lecture given by DR. G. DUNN, in his native Town of Barnsley, in Aid of a Fund for the Relief of the Surviving Sufferers by the Explosion which occurred at Warren Vale Colliery, on the morning of December 20th, 1851.]

——o——

THE PIT BOY.

The sun is sinking fast, mother,
  Behind yon far blue hills,
The signal bell has ceased, mother,
  The breeze of evening chills :
They call me to the pit, mother,
  The nightly toil to share :
One kiss before we part, mother,
  For danger lingers there.

My father's voice I hear, mother,
  As o'er his grave I tread,
He bade me cherish thee, mother,
  And share with thee, my bread :
And when I see thee smile, mother,
  My labour light shall be ;
And should his fate be mine, mother,
  Then heaven will comfort thee.

Nay, dry thy tearful eye, mother,
  I must not see thee weep ;
The Angels from on high, mother,
  O'er me their watch will keep.
Then oh ! farewell awhile, mother,
  My fervent prayer shall be,
Amidst those dangers dire, mother,
  That heaven may comfort thee.

PLATE No. 54